MW01399915

EARLY ONE-DESIGN SAILBOATS

EARLY ONE-DESIGN SAILBOATS

Grand old classes still active after half
a century and more

Diana Eames Esterly

Charles Scribner's Sons
New York

To Harry, with thanks for his criticism and patience

Copyright © 1979 by Diana Eames Esterly

Library of Congress Cataloging in Publication Data

Esterly, Diana Eames.
　　Early one-design sailboats.

　　Bibliography: p.131
　　1. Sailboats. 2. Boat-building—United
States—History. I. Title.
VM351.E83　　623.82'2　　79-13806
ISBN 0-684-16166-4

This book published simultaneously in the United States of America and in Canada - Copyright under the Berne Convention

All rights reserved. No part of this book may be reproduced in any form without the permission of Charles Scribner's Sons

1 3 5 7 9 11 13 15 17 19 M/C 20 18 16 14 12 10 8 6 4 2

Printed in the United States of America

Photographs by the author unless otherwise credited.
Book design and jacket design by the author.

CONTENTS

Introduction	vii
Acknowledgments	ix
The North Haven Dinghy	1
The San Francisco Bay Bird	6
The International Star	12
The Alden O Boat	18
The Wianno Senior	24
The Barnegat Bay Sneakbox	31
The Herreshoff 12½	38
The Dark Harbor 17½ (Manchester 17½, Bar Harbor 17½ and others)	44
The Beetle Cat	51
The Idem	56
The 18′ (Cape Cod Baby) Knockabout	61
The Northeast Harbor A (Eastern Yacht Club 17′ Gaff-rigged Sloop Knockabout Class)	68
The SS	75
The Cotuit Skiff	81
The Luedtke Catboat	88
The Herreshoff S	95
The Massachusetts Bay Hustler	100
The Inland Lake Scows	106
The Herreshoff 15 (Buzzards Bay 15, Watch Hill 15)	114
Other Early One-Design Classes	123
Glossary	127
Bibliography	131

INTRODUCTION

This book is a series of articles on a selection of early one-design sailboat classes designed and built prior to 1925. Most of the classes included are still actively racing today. However, this book is not intended to be an all-inclusive collection of still active pre-1925 classes.

According to the principle of one-design, all boats of a class are identical. They are built to the same specifications. Winning a race thus largely depends on a skipper's ability. In actuality, classes vary considerably in the degree to which they adhere to strict one-design principles. The boats in some classes, such as the Beetle Cat, are identical. In other classes, such as the 18' (Cape Cod Baby) Knockabout, adjustment and experimentation within limitations is, and always has been, permitted to everything but the hull. In yet other classes such as the Cotuit Skiff, the boats vary because they have been constructed by various builders over the years, often even of different materials.

The one-design concept evolved in the late 1800s and early 1900s. It was not strictly an American concept. Several classes, including the 13' Water Wag (first raced at Dun Laoghaire, Ireland, in 1887) were known in the British Isles before 1900. Prior to its inception in the United States, small boat racing had consisted primarily of contests between the existent work boats. The one-design principle won enthusiastic support during the first quarter of the twentieth century, and hundreds of classes were designed and built. There were, and still are, many reasons for its popularity. It eliminated handicapping, an unwieldy, often unfair system. One-design boats were less expensive because a number could be built at the same time. They did not become obsolete so rapidly. Sailing skill became more important than wealth or ingenuity for boat building.

Many of the early one-design classes came from the drawing boards of the most famous designers—Herreshoff, Crowninshield, Boardman, Alden, Mower, and others. The boats were constructed of the finest materials, by builders noted for their fine craftsmanship. Many, built of wood, perhaps antiquated by today's standards and expensive and time-consuming to keep up, are still lovingly sailed and maintained. Others are now made of fiberglass. Some have been changed drastically to reflect modern ideas. All have withstood the tests of time and are a tribute to their designers and to a different age. One wonders how many contemporary designs will survive 50 years and more.

I cannot vouch for the accuracy of every detail in this book. Much of the information came to me by letter or word of mouth. Memories are often inaccurate. Wherever possible I have tried to verify facts. Perhaps in the next few years a Yachting Museum will be established which will make a task such as writing this book less formidable. There is a real need for such if we are to adequately preserve our yachting history. In the meantime, for these early one-design classes, this is a beginning.

D. E. E.
March 1979

ACKNOWLEDGMENTS

It is only with much help from many individuals that I have been able to write this book, particularly since the histories of many of the classes included have never been thoroughly documented before. I would like to thank the following individuals for their outstanding help: Annetta S. Horton (SS), John B. Trevor, Jr. (Idem), Wilton B. (Bill) Crosby, Jr. (Wianno Senior), Leo Telesmanick (Beetle Cat), Webster Collins (18' Cape Cod Baby Knockabout), Anna M. Murray (Cotuit Skiff), Henry G. (Bud) Welsh and Bruce Whyte (Massachusetts Bay Hustler), Pemberton Drinker (Barnegat Bay Sneakbox), Barbara Lannon (North Haven Dinghy), Todd Cozzens and C. Stanley Ogilvy (Star), William G. Harding (Herreshoff 12½), Edward R. Welles III (Northeast Harbor A), Robert B. Rice (Dark Harbor 17½ and Northeast Harbor A), Steve Schneider (San Francisco Bay Bird), Raymond Coleman, David Cheever, Hubbard Phelps, and Augustin H. (Tony) Parker (Herreshoff 15), George W. Hanson and Ken Upham (Herreshoff S), Terrence G. Bischoff (Inland Lake Scows), and Eugene T. Connolly and Evers Bentner (Marblehead classes).

Thanks also to Dixie Clark for her editorial and production assistance.

Lastly, I would like to thank my father, Albert M. Eames, who spent untold hours in his darkroom helping me to print the photographs for this book, and provided unending support.

The North Haven Dinghy

The North Haven Dinghy is considered to be the first one-design class to appear in the United States. Amazingly, it is still racing today, making it the oldest active class as well. Fifteen or twenty of these pretty 14½' dinghies still go out to race in Fox Island Thorofare, between North Haven and Vinalhaven Islands in Maine's beautiful Penobscot Bay, as they have been doing for nearly a century, since 1885.

In the early 1880s North Haven was just beginning to develop into a popular summer community that would include such prominent names as Rockefeller, Saltonstall, Watson, and Morrow. The first residents were quick to discover the value of small craft for picnicking and exploring the rocky coves and shore. When William F. Weld arrived with cruising parties on board his yacht, *Gitana*, the local sailing craft were borrowed and informal racing became a natural pastime. Two of the first dinghies were built by a local carpenter, Henry Calderwood. After the *Gitana* tender was tried out and proved to do well against the competition, Dr. Charles G. Weld, William's brother, decided to have four matching dinghies built. These were constructed over the winter by J. O. Brown Boatyard of North Haven, and were raced the summer of 1885. Thus, the North Haven Dinghy was by some years the earliest one-design to appear.

A "Grand Dinghy Race" was held in August, 1887. To the chagrin of the two male competitors, Dr. Weld in Tucker Daland's *T.D.* and Charles K. Cobb in an unnamed dinghy, the race was won by a woman, Miss Ellen Hayward, in *Guffin*, owned by Alfred Bowditch. Apparently, Dr. Weld and Mr. Cobb engaged in a luffing match while the inexperienced Miss Hayward won the race. In the grandiloquent manner of the day, the popular Miss Hayward was presented a "diamond brooch" (some accounts say a sloop named *Wayward*).

The North Haven Dinghy is a 14'5½" catboat with 4'11" beam, and 13½" draft with the centerboard up and 3'10" with board down. It carries 118 sq. ft. of sail with two sets of reef points and no battens. The original design went through minor modifications including the replacement of the sprit-sail with a gaff rig, and the addition of more hull freeboard. The first dinghies had no flotation. The story goes that William Weld felt it wasn't necessary for the qualified sailor, but when his dinghy was the first to capsize and sink, air tanks were soon added. The model which became standard was taken from an early dinghy named *Elfin*. Around 1920 John G. Alden drew up a set of construction drawings using lines taken off the dinghy *Kidozo*. A proposed Marconi rig was included as well as the gaff rig. These plans were revised in 1929 and have been used ever since. The wood dinghies are framed in oak and planked in ½" finished cedar with

The start of the Pulpit Harbor Race.

Anne White photo/ reprinted with permission from *Down East* Magazine, Camden, Maine

Anne White

oak garboards and top strake. The keel, skeg, stem and centerboard are of oak. Fastenings are copper rivets over copper burrs. There are 6 lbs. of lead on the centerboard and 350 lbs. of inside ballast. The boats are heavily and well built and thus hold their shape.

The dinghies became so popular that during the 1920s and 1930s they raced in two divisions. In the past few years about eight fiberglass boats have been built. They race competitively with the wooden dinghies, about ten of which have been built since 1960 by J. O. Brown, the original boatyard, and another builder, Y–Knot Industries. These two yards have also finished off some of the fiberglass boats.

Today the dinghies still race out of the North Haven Casino (an accredited yacht club) in two classes—the adults, and the midgets for children. There is a July series and a separate August series so those with only one month of vacation may participate. The adults are divided into divisions racing on Mondays and Saturdays. The midgets race Wednesday and Saturday mornings. In the adult class, boats are scored by awarding one point for every boat beaten. The boat with the highest number of points wins the series. In the midget class points are awarded to the skipper, not the boat.

Anne White

There are four special races each season: the Fourth of July Race, the Labor Day Race, the Mill River Race and the Pulpit Harbor Race. The Mill River Race sends the dinghies up a narrow, rockbound river where the tide and current must be reckoned with to avoid ending up on the rocks. In the Pulpit Harbor Race the dinghies go around the western end of North Haven Island to Pulpit Harbor on the north side.

The North Haven Dinghy is not only fast, but wet and tricky to handle downwind. With a sea running, sailing before the wind requires great concentration. The crew must sit well aft to keep the bow from burying itself. The North Haven Dinghies adhere to strick one-design principles. No modifications are permitted. No doubt the great sport of racing them and the challenge it represents has a good deal to do with the popularity of this fine little boat now in its ninth decade.

Anne White photo / reprinted with permission from *Down East* Magazine, Camden, Maine

Courtesy John G. Alden, Inc.

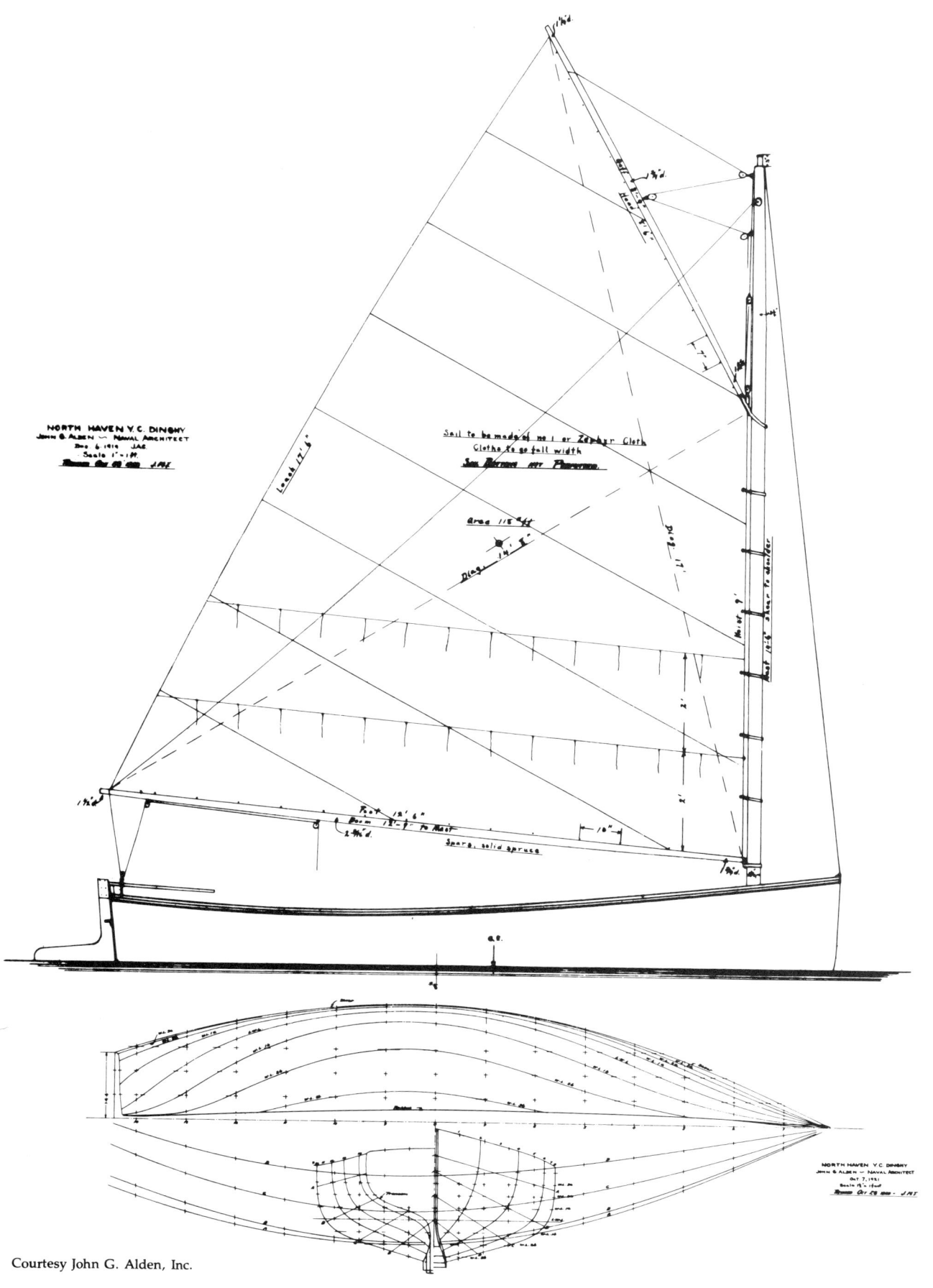

5

The San Francisco Bay Bird

The San Francisco Bay Bird is a one-design for the best skippers, for those who appreciate a challenging boat, one that is tough to race well. The challenge the Bird presents, together with the fact that the boat is so aptly suited to the windy, choppy conditions of San Francisco Bay (for which she was specifically designed) has contributed greatly to the enduring popularity of the class. Today fourteen or fifteen Birds still turn out for the summer race series. Out of the original twenty-six boats that were built, twenty-three are still sailing, an outstanding percentage considering that most of these boats are fifty years old.

Though the origin of the San Francisco Bay Bird is somewhat obscure, it appears that Fred Brewer of the Madden and Lewis yard, Sausalito, California, drew up the plans for and built the first Bird, *Osprey*, for members of the San Francisco Yacht Club in 1922. The Club members accepted the design, but sent the plans to John G. Alden in Boston for his suggestions on modification. Alden's recommendation for the addition of ballast to the keel was accepted, but other suggestions were overruled. Birds numbers 2 and 3, *Curlew* and *Betty* (later renamed *Kookabura*), were soon built at Madden's yard. In 1927, after five Birds had been constructed, the Pacific Coast Yachting Association sponsored the Bird Class during its 1927 meeting. As a result of this endorsement, a committee was appointed to promote the class on the Coast. More than twenty additional Birds were built, most of them in the 1920s. The last Bird was built in the late 1930s. Each carries the birds' wings insignia on the mainsail and the name of a bird on the transom.

Of the total of twenty-six Birds, only three are missing today. *Osprey*, as the story goes, was stolen by an escaped convict who sailed her outside the Golden Gate and up the coast to Bolinas, where he ran her up on the rocks. The two other missing hulls, numbers 14 and 15, were assigned to boats to be built in Southern California. There is no record that they were ever launched. It may well be that twenty-three or twenty-four Birds are still afloat.

At first glance, the design specifications for the Bird seem ordinary enough. She is a raised-deck sloop of 30'1" overall, and 24'3" on the waterline, with a 7'8" beam, and draft of 5'3". She is framed in white oak and planked in Oregon pine, with a canvased deck and teak or mahogany wash rails. Her spar is fir or pine. She has a small cabin with two settee berths, and head. It is only when one considers the ballast-displacement ratio and the rig that the kind of boat the Bird is begins to become apparent. She displaces 9,000 lbs., and of this 3,600 lbs. is outside, or keel ballast. In addition, 1,000 lbs. of internal ballast is often placed around the base of the mast, bringing the total ballast to about 4,600 lbs., a 50 percent

Diane Beeston

or better ballast-displacement ratio. The rig has an exceptionally low aspect ratio of about 3 to 2. The mast is 33' above the deck and the boom, which extends over the stern, is more than 20' long. The mast is placed well forward in the boat (⅓ to ⅔ ratio). Of the 408 sq. ft. of sail area, the mainsail is the driving sail, and the small, club-footed jib is considered a balancing sail. The 50 percent ballast-displacement ratio and the low-aspect rig combine to make the Bird very stiff. The hull goes through the plentiful chop of San Francisco Bay instead of over it. The internal ballast is well forward, holding the bow down in the chop. She is at her best in the prevalent twenty-five to forty-knot winds.

"Nothing sails like a Bird." This, the motto of the San Francisco Bird Association, is most definitely true. Certainly the design is not typical of that of other early one-designs of similar size, at least when it comes to ballast-displacement ratio and rig. In the usual windy conditions of San Francisco Bay the Bird is fast and maneuverable. She will stand up and

Diane Beeston

Diane Beeston

take what the Bay has to offer without reefing. (There are no reef points in her mainsail, proving the trust Bird owners have in their boats.) There are many wild tales, most of them true, of Birds carrying on in forty and fifty-knot winds, surging along to finish well ahead of larger craft, while other boats are dismasted or sunk in what has come to be called "Birdboat weather." In the occasional light air she is fast enough so that her limited sail inventory of main, jib, and spinnaker are adequate. There is plenty to keep both skipper and crew alert: the Bird is wet and uncomfortable; the low boom is a constant threat and obstructs vision; the running backstays must be tended to keep the mast in the boat; and the forestay must be released and secured at the mast when the spinnaker is set (and *resecured* forward when the spinnaker is doused before a windward leg).

The first San Francisco Bay Birds were built for around $2,000 each. At this writing, the selling range is $6,000 to $10,000 depending on the boat's condition. To build a new one would probably cost around $30,000. The idea of building a fiberglass Bird has been considered, or at least suggested. But Bird owners are repelled by the thought. In all likelihood, too few could be sold to make it economically feasible anyway.

The San Francisco Bay Birds, fifty years of age and more, carry on. They are a uniquely effective design for a specific environment. It is no surprise that many of San Francisco's top skippers have raced Birds at one time or another, nor that Bird racing inspires some of the Bay's keenest competition. The Birds have been around San Francisco Bay and the Golden Gate longer than the bridge has!

Diane Beeston

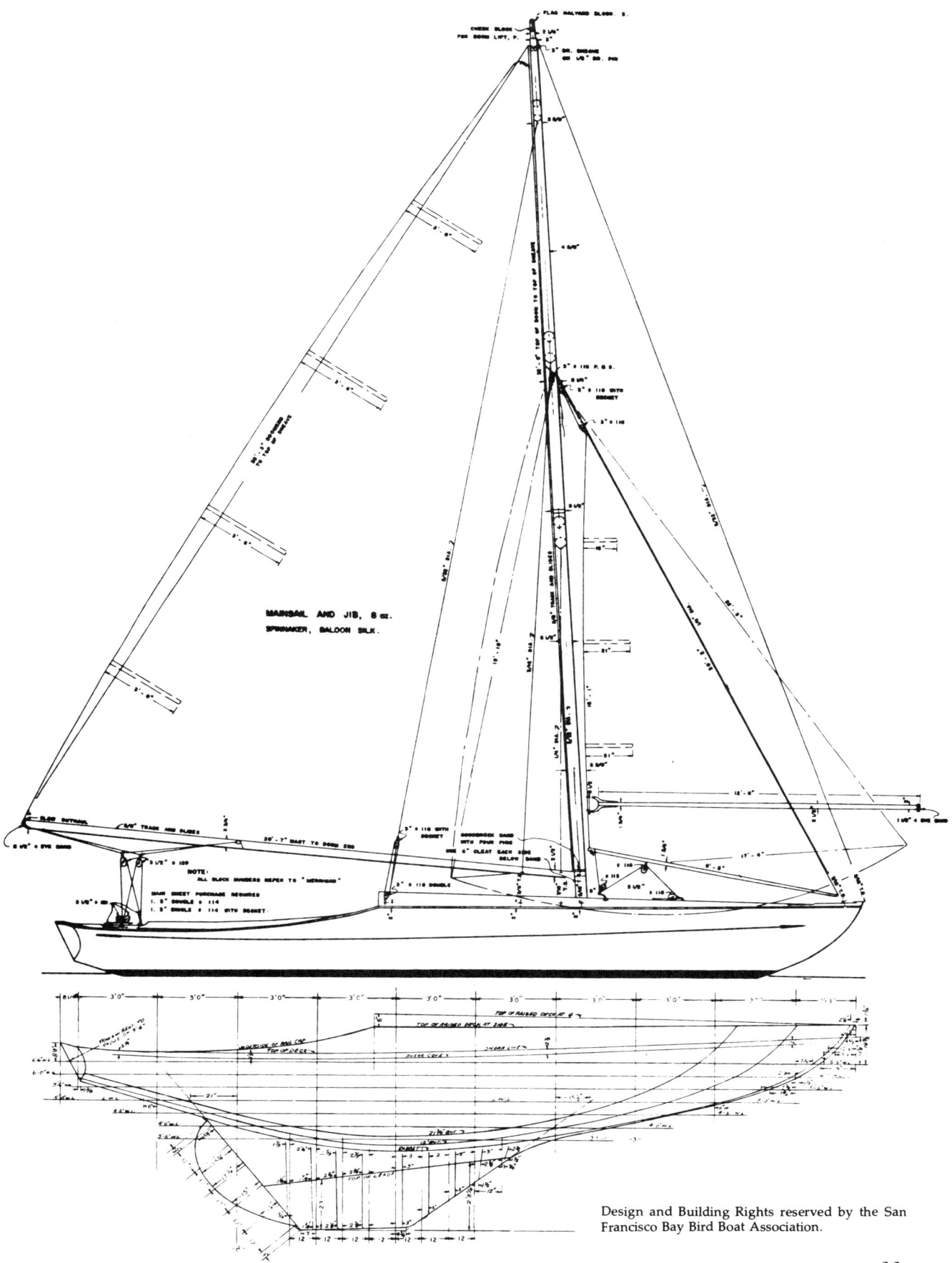

Design and Building Rights reserved by the San Francisco Bay Bird Boat Association.

11

The International Star

Looking at the Star today, it is hard to believe that she is one of the earliest one-designs. A finely tuned modern racing machine, it seems incredible that her hull design has remained unchanged since 1911. It is surely a tribute to her designer, to the Star Class organization, and to those who have sailed her through the years that she has evolved into what she is today.

The Star is by far the most well known of the early one-designs, and for that matter, all classes, new as well as old. Numbering over 6,000 boats in twenty-seven countries, it is one of the largest classes in the world. The International Star Class Yacht Racing Association was the first one-design class organization to be founded. The first and for many years, the only, international one-design racing class, the Star will have been an Olympic Class continuously from 1932–1980, with the exception of 1976.

The Star Class history really began in 1906 when George "Pop" Corry asked his friend and fellow sailor, the well known yacht designer William Gardner, to draw up a small one-design that would not only be fast and stable, but inexpensive to produce. The Bug, an 18' keel sloop which Gardner designed, although inexpensive proved to be too small and wet, and in 1910 Corry requested a larger version. Francis Sweisguth, a designer in Gardner's firm, drew up the plans for the Star. Twenty-two boats were built by Ike Smith at Port Washington, Long Island, New York. They raced for the first time at the Memorial Day Regatta May 30, 1911, at the Harlem Yacht Club.

The Star hull measures 22'8¼" overall, 15'6" on the waterline, has a beam of 5'8¼", and a draft of 3'6". It has hard chines, low freeboard, and a fin keel carrying a 900 lb. cast iron bulb. The cockpit is small, allowing space (while racing at least) for only the skipper and one crew member. The original rig was gaff, or sliding gunter, with the gaff almost vertically parallel to the mast. The boom overhung the stern by 3'. In 1921 the rig was changed to a short Marconi. The sail shape remained the same, however, and it was even possible to use old sails. In 1929 the overhanging boom was shortened, and the rig went from low- to high-aspect ratio with a taller Marconi mainsail.

As George Corry is called the "Father of the Stars," his friend, George Elder was the father of the Star Class Association. He bought a Star in 1914, and in 1916 presented the novel idea of a class organization to the other Star owners. Elder visualized fleets not only in the harbors of Long Island Sound, but all over the country and eventually the world, and he proposed a class association to administer their affairs and interfleet racing. It is difficult today to realize just how farsighted this idea was. For the most part, individual yacht clubs had their own one-design classes, dif-

Star Class Races in front of the Malecon at Havana, Cuba, during March 1929. Note overhanging booms.

José Luis López Gómez photo/courtesy ISCYRA

Stars racing today.

Courtesy ISCYRA

13

George Elder at the helm.

Ernest Tanare photo/courtesy ISCYRA

ferent from those of the other clubs. Not only were there no class organizations; there were no interclub races. Even if the boats had been similar, their owners were limited by the distance they could sail, or be towed, to another club. The automobile was new and the possibility of transporting a boat by trailer from place to place was practically inconceivable.

Elder's plan was finally adopted January 20, 1922 at a meeting at the Astor Hotel in New York City. By this time 110 Stars had been built and it seemed more probable that an organization might succeed. George Corry was the first president, but Elder replaced him in 1924, and went on to run the organization for the next twenty-five years. His methods of accomplishing things no doubt seemed high-handed to many, but his efforts were largely responsible for the strong organization of today. The Association published its first yearbook in 1922 and first rules in 1923. It is remarkable how many of these rules have survived to this day. The class magazine *Starlights* was first published in 1925. The Association is also responsible for the class committee concept of conducting races. Since 1927 races have been sponsored by various clubs, but are always conducted by a Star Class Association Committee, according to strict Star rules and regulations.

Racing spread early from Long Island Sound to Narragansett Bay, and Lake Erie and the Detroit River. In 1922, the Stars raced for the first time

Courtesy ISCYRA

1976 Bacardi Cup Races.

on the West Coast at Los Angeles. The first National Championship took place in 1922. The class became international in 1923 when a fleet was established at Vancouver, British Columbia, and the first World Championship was held that year. Today there are district and continental, as well as fleet championships.

A lot has happened to the Star since George Corry and George Elder sailed her. In the 1930s Walther von Hutschler of Germany came up with the flexible rig. Duarte Bello of Portugal provided automatic bailers and circular vang tracks in the 1950s. Hiking straps have long been in use. Fiberglass was approved for hull construction in 1966, and aluminum for the spars in 1971. The fittings are all of the latest design. Everything is adjustable. The Star rigging is very responsive to tuning and it has been the intention of the Class Association that this be the case. The hull dimensions are strictly determined, but the rigging and fittings, beyond having fixed major dimensions, are left open to the individual. This has resulted in continued evolution, and has undoubtedly presented the challenge which has drawn so many of the world's greatest yachtsmen to this fine boat.

Chris Caswell photo/courtesy ISCYRA

Courtesy ISCYRA

The Alden O Boat

It was with practicality in mind that John Alden designed his O Boat in 1922. The boat was intended primarily for young people; to be used in teaching them how to sail, to be raced and even owned by them. The boat had to be safe and economical. It also had to be fast enough to provide good sport. Alden's O Boat met these criteria and the design had widespread and lasting appeal. It is raced to this day on Upper St. Regis Lake in the Adirondack Mountains of New York.

It was a group of Marblehead yachtsmen who commissioned John Alden to design a boat for the young sailors of Marblehead between the ages of twelve and eighteen. These yachtsmen were concerned about the lack of interest in sailing among the young people at that time. They felt that it might be due in part to the fact that, always serving as crew for their fathers, they were never given the chance to act independently. No doubt these men also realized the valuable lessons in store for the youngsters as they learned to sail, raced, and owned their own boats.

To be economical the boat could not be too large. But it couldn't be too small, because in addition to being safe for the children, the adults had stipulated that the boat be one that they might occasionally take outside the protected harbor into rougher waters! (Apparently, in spite of their altruistic intentions, they couldn't resist getting into the act!) So the O Boat was designed with a maximum of waterline length for her overall length to provide the most boat for the money. The original cost was $600, sails included.

In the interests of economy and versatility the design called for a centerboard instead of a keel. The centerboard was slightly cheaper to construct, and made the boat considerably cheaper to haul out and store. Alden, with an eye to the future no doubt, also realized that a centerboard design could be used in a variety of places and would make the boat easier and cheaper to ship.

For safety's sake the hull was designed with considerable beam to give it stability. A watertight bulkhead or tanks forward made the boat virtually unsinkable. In the interest of comfort, as well as safety, Alden designed the boat with a maximum of freeboard and a deep cockpit well aft so that the skipper and crew were generally dry.

A number of boats were delivered to Marblehead for the 1922 season. Known as the O Fifteen Footers, they were quite popular throughout the twenties. As many as sixteen turned out for the starts in 1923, and twenty-two in 1924. Curiously, along in the late twenties, when the class was at its peak with twenty-five normally starting, a squall capsized many of the boats and their popularity began to fade. Their numbers dwindled to eight and then to zero by 1931.

John B. Trevor, Jr. photo

A second version of the O Boat design was developed by Alden, with differences principally in beam, ballast and sail area. This boat was slightly shorter, had a greater beam, more ballast, and less sail area, all of which combined to make a slower, more stable boat than the first design. It seems likely that the original design used in Marblehead and elsewhere proved too tender for some areas and Alden designed the second version to be more stable.

One version or the other of the Alden O Boat became popular in many places including South Boston, Cohasset, Hingham, New Bedford, South Dartmouth, Nonquit, Wellfleet, and Rockport, as well as Marblehead, in Massachusetts; Watch Hill, in Rhode Island; Cedarhurst, Port Jefferson, and Upper St. Regis Lake, in New York, and Prouts Neck, Northeast Harbor and Blue Hill, in Maine. On Long Island Sound the second design was popular as the JA class. By 1930 over 250 Os had been built by several builders including Graves, Chamberlain, and George Chaisson. Although the class dwindled out in Marblehead, between 7 and 13 Os from other Massachusetts yacht clubs continued to race in the midsummer Race Week at least into the mid 1930s.

The specifications for the two versions of Alden O Boat are as follows (version two in parentheses): length overall 18'3" (18'1"); waterline length 15'6" (15'5"); beam 6'2" (6'8"); draft 11" (11½"); inside ballast 450 lbs. (550 lbs.); total weight 1,800 lbs. (2,000 lbs.), sail area 200 sq. ft. (192 sq. ft.). The rig was Marconi and the change in sail area was in the mainsail only. The jib and spinnaker were the same on both designs. Sometimes the

Os start a race on Upper St. Regis Lake.

John B. Trevor, Jr. photo

version one sail plan was used with the version two hull, a more powerful combination. The boats were framed in oak and generally planked in white pine or cedar.

It is the second version of John Alden's O Boat design which is still raced today on Upper St. Regis Lake, New York. The boats first appeared around 1925. Eventually, twenty-one were purchased. They have proved popular with young and old alike. Sixteen of the original twenty-one have been raced in the last five years and only one is irretrievably lost. Not a bad record for boats of fifty years plus!

John B. Trevor, Jr. photo

John B. Trevor, Jr. photo

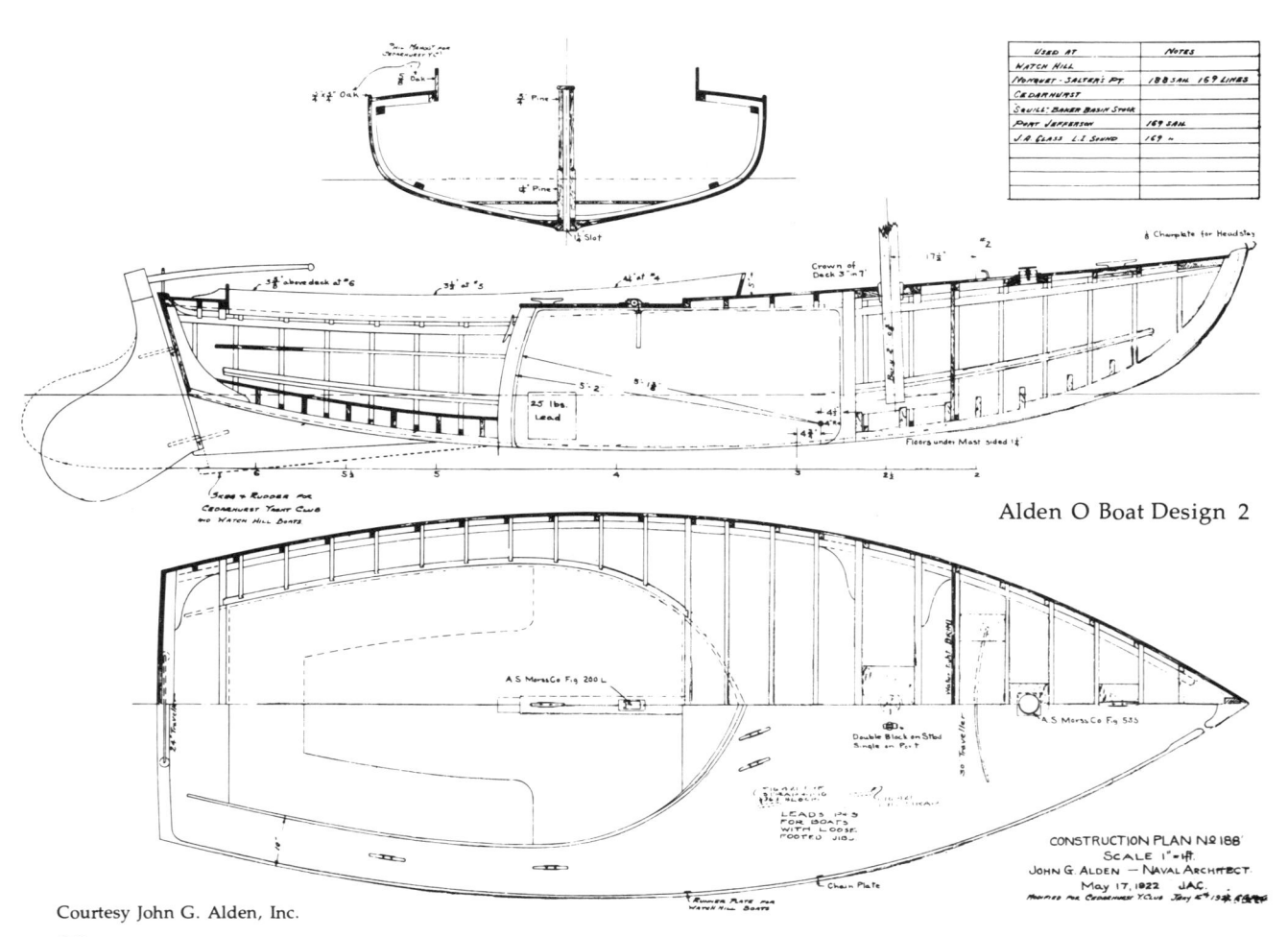

Alden O Boat Design 2

Courtesy John G. Alden, Inc.

22

Courtesy John G. Alden, Inc.

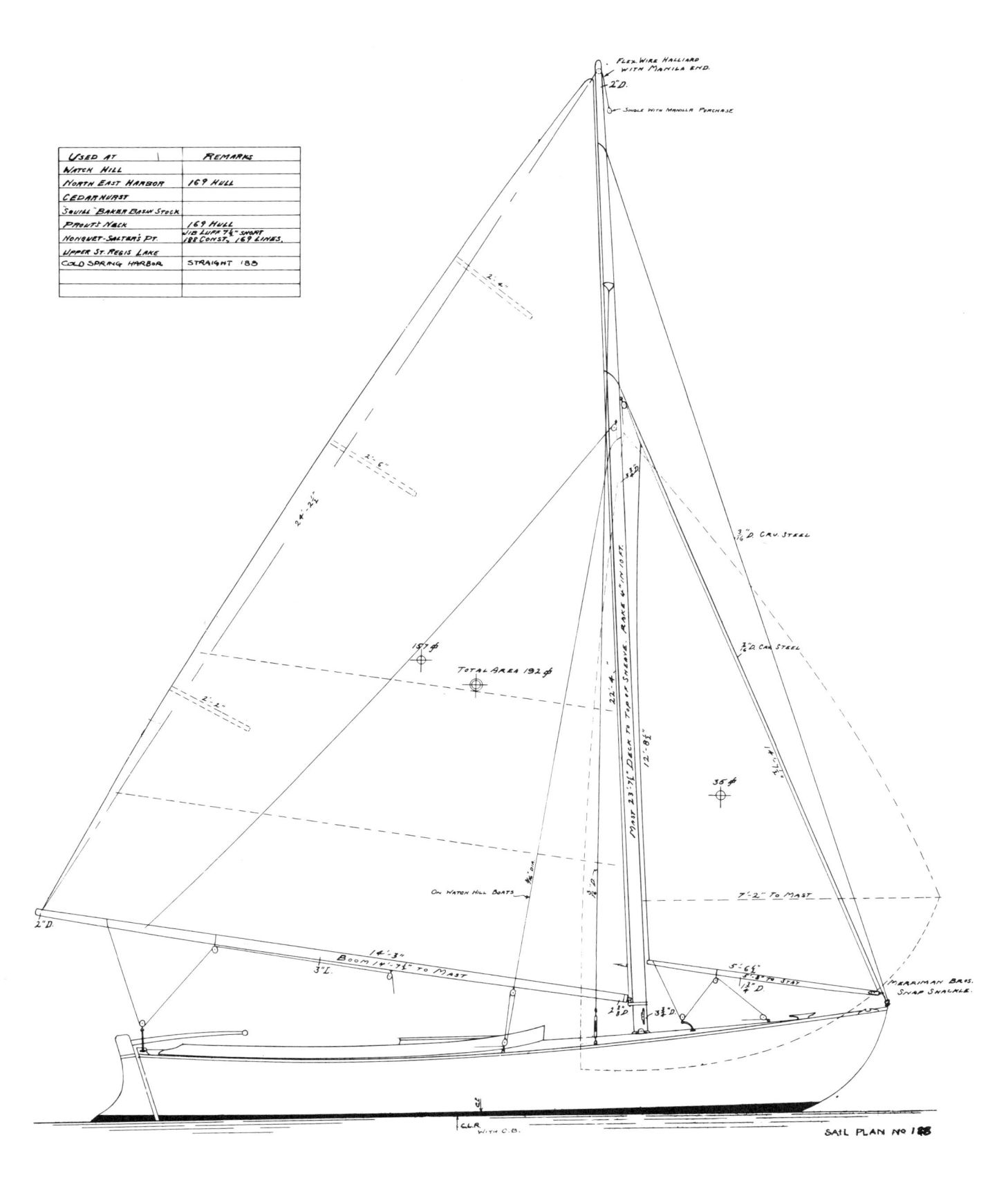

23

The Wianno Senior

Of the early one-design sailboats, the Wianno Senior is remarkable in several ways. There are probably more Wianno Seniors still actively racing than any other class constructed of wood and of similar size (25' overall, 17'6" waterline). In addition, the Senior is still gaff-rigged, and new boats have been built recently (four in 1976).

In the fall of 1913 members of thirteen old sailing families of Wianno, Massachusetts, on Cape Cod got together and commissioned H. Manley Crosby of Crosby Yacht Building and Storage Company to design and build them a small yacht for racing. The Crosby family had been building boats for many years and was famous for its Cape Cod Catboats (Crosby Cats). The boat which Mr. Crosby came up with is one of the reasons for the long lived popularity of the Wianno Senior Class. The keel-centerboard design is well suited to sail in the shallow waters of Nantucket Sound, on the south side of the Cape, where constantly shifting shoals, tricky currents, and strong tides create a steep chop to run in against the wind. With board up she draws 2'6" and can skim over the shoals. With board down she draws 5'6". Stability comes from 600 lbs. of iron on the bottom of the keel, 600 lbs. of lead ballast inside, the wide centerboard, and 8' beam. In addition, her heaviness and gaff rig driver her well to windward in short, steep waves when the wind is blowing hard—conditions in which a light boat is slowed. The Wianno Senior design has remained virtually unchanged because there has been no need for change.

Thirteen boats were built in 1913 for the 1914 season. The Crosby family (H. Manley, then his sons Malcolm, Carroll, Wilton B., and Horace, and grandsons Bradford, Wilton B., Jr., Theodore, and Malcolm M.) has continuously built the Seniors ever since, with the exception of the war years and 1952 to 1962. About 160 boats have been built (although hull numbers are in the 170s due to renumbering). H. Manley Crosby used a half model from which he constructed a mold to the full dimensions. Plans were not drawn up until 1930. Stem, keel and framing was, and still is, of white oak. The first 100 boats were planked in cypress. Since 1935, starting with number 101, the boats have been planked in mahogany—first Philippine then Honduran. Fastenings were originally galvanized boat nails. Since 1932, starting with number 98, they have been Everdur bronze screws covered with wooden bungs of mahogany. Originally, the curved forward part of the cabin trunk was a single piece of steam-bent oak. It was later replaced with mahogany and is now laminated mahogany. In 1927 the rudder was extended to the depth of the keel.

The Wianno Senior carries 366 sq. ft. of sail (a 294' gaff-rigged main and a 72' jib). Marconi rigs were designed by John Alden and Sparkman

Marna, number 120, owned and sailed by John T. Fallon.

and Stephens, but they never caught on. The gaff is apparently superior for the conditions in which the boats sail. A single luff spinnaker with a 14' pole was added in 1928. It was used until 1961, when the class changed to a parachute spinnaker with a 9' pole. Some change for racing has been made in the rig over the years. Backstays were added. An adjustable track and slide is now used for the jib sheet leads instead of fixed leads. The backstays have a track and slide instead of a tackle.

At first, the Seniors racing out of the Wianno Yacht Club had different size sails and sometimes raced with other kinds of boats. The design became standardized by the early 1930s when the class became so popular it spread to yacht clubs at Hyannis Port, Bass River, and Harwich Port (Stone Horse). The boats still race out of these four clubs. There are also a few at Scituate, Massachusetts. During the 1920s as many as thirty boats would race. In the thirties, the thirty-five to forty boats which were raced were divided into two divisions. The class has continued strong since,

Wianno Seniors racing in the 1930s.

Photo by Crosby Yacht Building and Storage Co.

Wianno Seniors racing today.

with minor ups and downs. Today thirty to thirty-five boats are often at the starting line for interclub races.

In addition to club racing, a series of six regattas are raced between the four clubs. These include the Wianno to Edgartown Long Distance Race, the Edgartown Regatta, and four races at the different clubs. The Long Distance Race Challenge Cup is awarded to the winner of the Wianno to Edgartown Race. The Frederic F. Scudder Memorial Trophy goes to the boat and skipper with the most points in the interclub races. The second highest scorer is awarded the H. Manley Crosby Memorial Trophy.

In 1932 Joseph P. Kennedy bought number 94, *Victura.* It was in this boat that President John F. Kennedy sailed and raced. At the time of the Fiftieth Anniversary Regatta in 1964, number 132, *Resolute,* owned by Robert F. Kennedy (and still owned by his wife, Ethel) was launched. Eunice K. Shriver bought number 139, *Head Start,* in 1967, and Edward M. Kennedy had a new *Victura* built in 1975. The original *Victura* will be part of the Kennedy Memorial Library collection.

Dorothy I. Crossley

Courtesy Crosby Yacht, Inc.

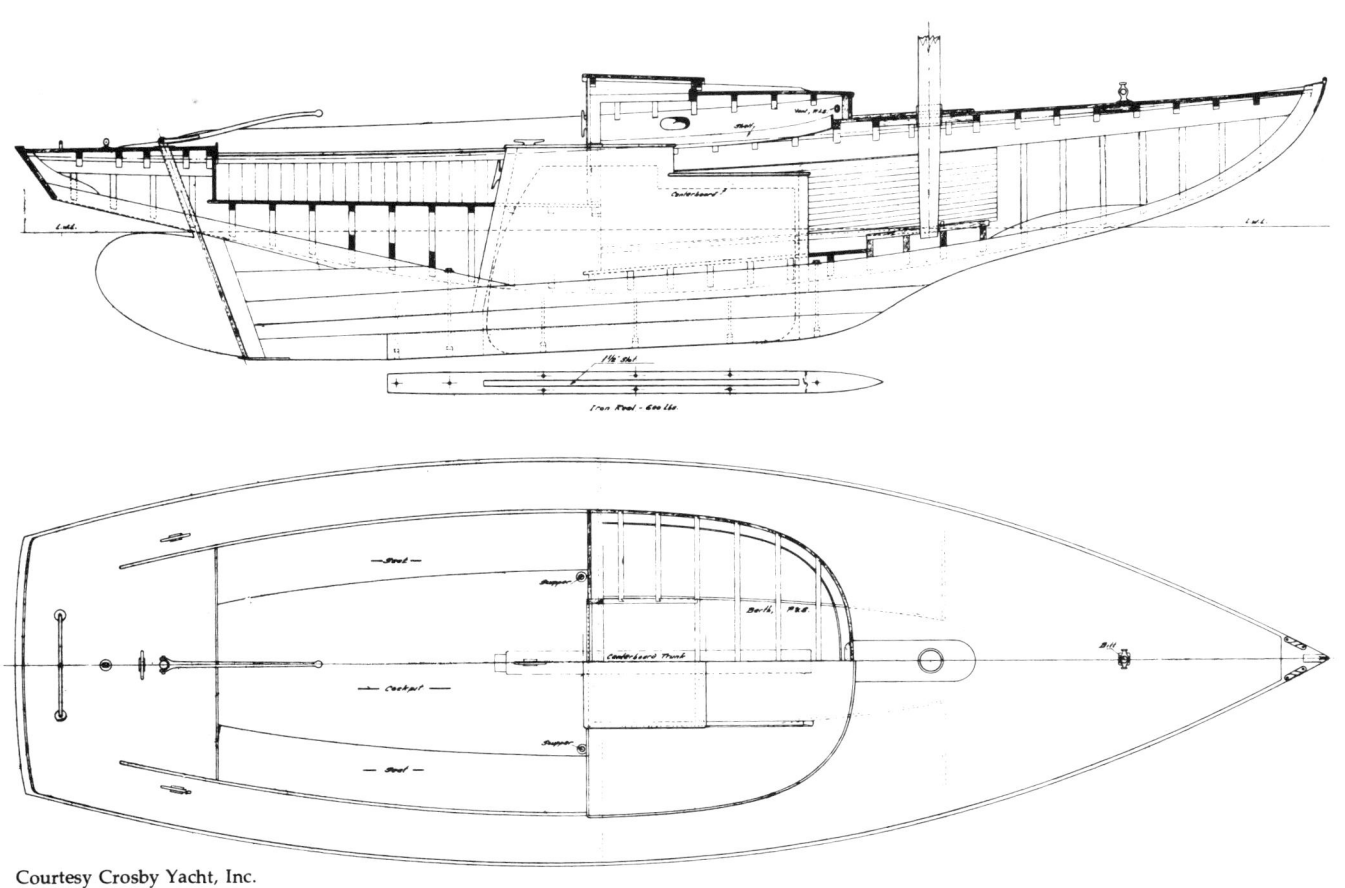

In 1965, James G. Hinkle donated number 11, *Fantasy*, to Mystic Seaport Museum. He had owned and raced her for fifty-one years. She won her first race in 1915 and the Stone Horse Regatta in 1964—and lots of others in between. Certainly this record says a lot about the Wianno Senior.

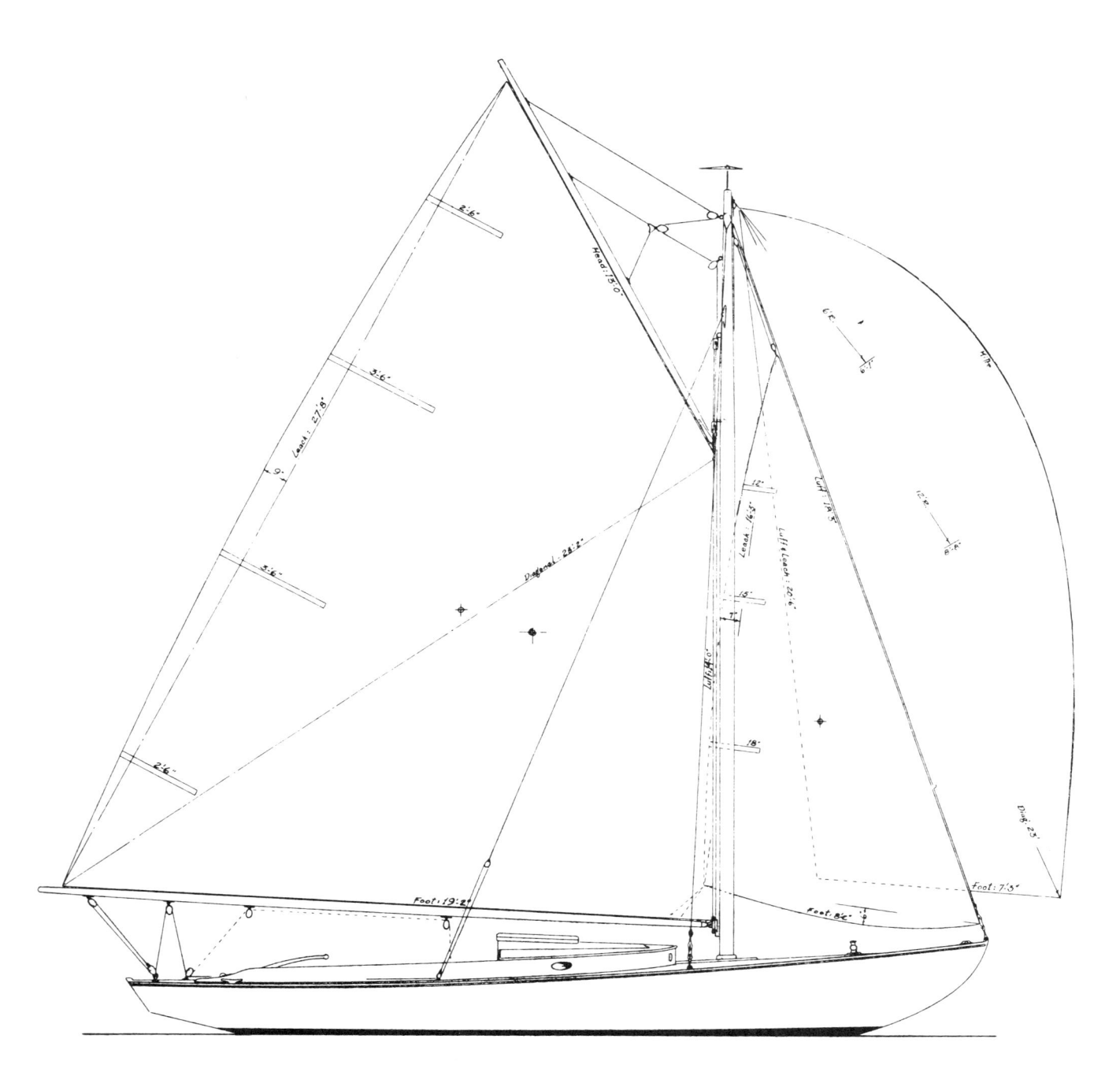

Courtesy Crosby Yacht, Inc.

The Barnegat Bay Sneakbox

The history of the Barnegat Bay Sneakboxes is intriguing. They have been built in various sizes and have had numerous designers and builders. Their origins go back to the 1830s, although they didn't really get going as one-design classes until the 1920s. The hull design is directly descended from the gunning sneakbox, the first of which is alleged to have been designed and built in 1836 by Hazelton Seaman of West Creek, New Jersey, near Tuckerton, in the southern reaches of Barnegat Bay.

The first sneakbox hulls were very similar to those of today's racing sneakboxes. The shape has been described as looking like two spoons, a shallow one upside down covering a deeper one. It is flat-bottomed with no discernable chine. It is beamy and shallow draft so that it moves over the water, not through it. The construction is unusual. Instead of a keel, there is a "set-up plank" the same thickness as the rest of the planking, to which the frames and vertical transom are attached. There is no stem. At the bow of the boat, joined to the end of the set-up plank and running back across the topside ends of the forward ribs are two pieces called harpings or harpins, which form the connection between deck and bottom. The planking, as well as the tongue and groove decking, runs parallel to the hull centerline, not parallel to the waterline, as with conventional planking.

The typical gunning sneakbox was 12' long, had a small, rectangular central cockpit with coaming and removable cover, a canvas spray shield forward, folding oarlocks for rowing, and often carried a sprit-sail. They were used as floating duck blinds in the marshes of New Jersey. Camouflaged with marsh grass, these low-freeboard craft enabled hunters to sneak up on their prey; hence the name, sneakbox.

In 1879 Nathaniel Bishop brought these boats to the attention of the public with his widely read book, *Four Months in a Sneakbox,* about his trip from Pittsburgh to Florida in a twelve footer grandly named the *Centennial Republic.* By the late 1880s the sailing qualities of the sneakboxes had been realized and they were racing informally on Barnegat Bay.

The first sneakboxes adapted for racing were not really one-designs, by the usual definition. They included an eighteen footer which became popular around 1890, a seventeen footer designed by E. B. Schock in 1902, and a 1906 class limited to not more than 20' in length (carrying a crew of six to eight, and eighteen to thirty-five 30 lb. sandbags). Probably the first one-design class was designed by Charles D. Mower in 1914. This twenty footer, compared with the earlier racing sneakboxes, was lighter, with a more rounded bow, flatter bottom, fuller bilges, and smaller gaff rig. In 1924 the rig became Marconi. This boat outperformed the earlier sneakboxes, and its reputation as the fastest boat on the bay was only ended by the introduction, in the mid-twenties, of the E Scows.

About 1918, J. Howard Perrine of Barnegat designed a 15' boat along the lines of a sneakbox which was destined to be the most popular of all the sneakbox classes. These boats, called Perrines, measured 15' overall and 13' on the waterline, with a 5'9" beam, 6" draft with swing centerboard up, 5' with centerboard down, and carried 156 sq. ft. of sail. The first boats sold for $225. In 1920 the Polyhue Yacht Club of Beachwood, New Jersey purchased 7 boats. According to Charles E. Lucke, Jr.,* this was the first one-design fleet with colored sails in the United States. The popularity of the fifteen footer grew rapidly. It was designated a class by the Barnegat Bay Yacht Racing Association in 1922, and by 1923 40 to 50 boats partici-

---

*Charles E. Lucke, Jr., "Fifteen-Foot Sneakboxes and Junior Sailing on Barnegat Bay," in *Sailing Craft,* ed. Edwin J. Schoettle (New York: The Macmillan Co., 1928) p. 612.

Courtesy William C. Schoettle

Early racing Sneakboxes at Bay Head Yacht Club about 1906.

pated in junior BBYRA racing events. Four hundred had been built by 1927 and eventually around 3,000 were built to be sailed in New Jersey and elsewhere, making it one of the largest one-design classes. Other builders included Eli Townsend, who built 25 boats for Seaside Park Yacht Club quite early, and Morton Johnson, Zack Johnson, and David Beaton

Fifteen-foot Sneakbox, known as a Perrine.

Asbury Park Press photo/George Tiedemann

Fifteen-foot Sneakboxes racing on Barnegat Bay.

Robert F. Morris

12' Sneakboxes race at Little Egg Harbor.

more recently. These boats are still officially listed as a class by the Barnegat Bay Yacht Racing Association, and a few continue to race.

In Little Egg Harbor, south of Barnegat Bay, a class of 12' one-design sneakboxes evolved from the nonstandard converted gunning boats which were raced there. These boats still race today, essentially unchanged from the 1930s. They are the only true sneakboxes racing in that they retain the removable unstayed sprit-sail rig and the daggerboard of the original gunning sneakbox. The latest wooden boats of this design, called Neffs, were

Robert F. Morris

Little Egg Harbor 12' Sneakbox.

35

built in the late fifties by Grellet-Gibbons Neff from plans drawn up from lines taken off an older fast boat. A fiberglass mold was developed by Charles Dore in the early sixties, and was used by him and later by Pacemaker in the seventies to produce fiberglass sneakboxes.

Other sneakbox design adaptations have been built. J. H. Perrine's short-lived 12' Butterfly is an example. Others are still active today. The Diamond, built by Perrine, Beaton, and Fitzpatrick, is raced at the Island Heights Yacht Club on the Toms River. Philip Clarke of Mantoloking designed a Marconi-rigged Duckboat in 1951 and he, and later David Beaton, built it. It is raced at Bay Head, Mantoloking, Manasquan River, and Island Heights Yacht Clubs. The Clarke boat has a higher crown deck and is thus distinguished from the Beaton version. Others include a fourteen footer, called the 8 Ball, a fifteen and one-half footer, and an eighteen footer by Allan Chadwick.

The sneakbox hull design has proved itself many times over. It is a durable, stable, seaworthy boat, excellent for teaching youngsters how to sail. When one looks at the sneakboxes row on row, at places such as Bay Head or Little Egg Harbor Yacht Clubs, there is no question—these boats will be around for a long time to come.

Duckboats at Bay Head Yacht Club.

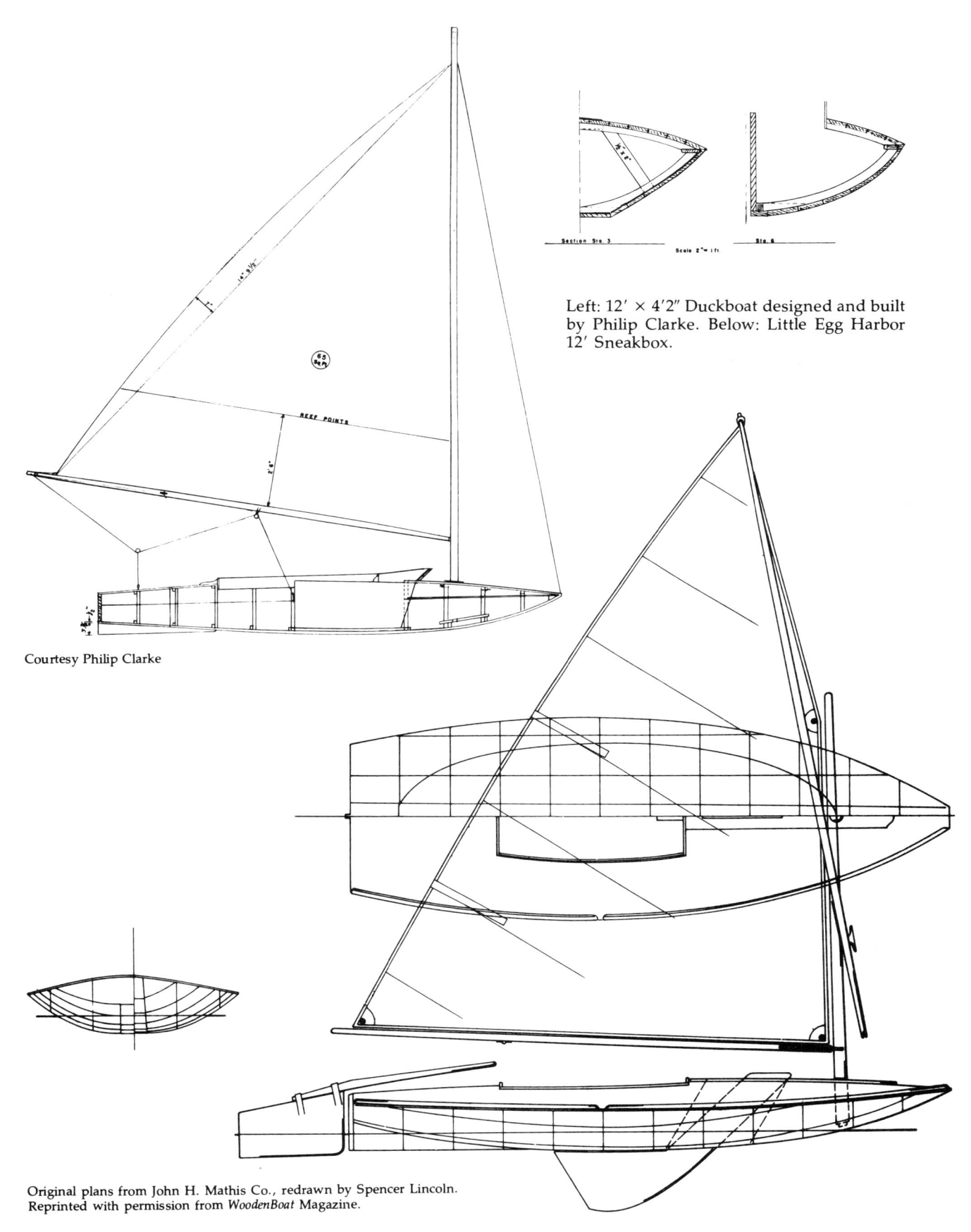

Left: 12′ × 4′2″ Duckboat designed and built by Philip Clarke. Below: Little Egg Harbor 12′ Sneakbox.

Courtesy Philip Clarke

Original plans from John H. Mathis Co., redrawn by Spencer Lincoln. Reprinted with permission from *WoodenBoat* Magazine.

37

The Herreshoff 12½

A classic has been defined as "A craft most representative of the excellence of vessel design, having recognized worth, generally combining beauty, utility, and seaworthy character in the design."* Surely this is an apt description of the Herreshoff 12½ (commonly called Herreshoff 12). A handsome keel sloop, the hull shape, usage of interior space, and the rig exemplify all the qualities of fine design. Measuring 12½' on the waterline, 15'10" overall with a beam of 5'10" and a draft of 2'6", it is noted for its excellent sailing characteristics, its speed and responsiveness. In addition, it is a good family boat because it is comfortable, easy to sail, seaworthy, and therefore safe.

Designed and built in 1914 by Nathaniel Greene Herreshoff at the request of Robert Emmons and friends from Monument Beach, Cape Cod, Massachusetts, 19 boats were commissioned in Buzzards Bay for the 1915 season. The boat became a rapid success. By the thirties, 300 boats were racing in Buzzards Bay. Thirty to 40 boats were at the starting line at each of five Massachusetts Yacht Clubs: Beverly (at Marion), The Buzzards (at Cataumet), Mattapoisett, Nonquitt, and Quissett. The Beverly Club sported 75 boats in 1937. Popularity spread to Narragansett Bay, Rhode Island; Marblehead, Massachusetts; Fishers Island, and Long Island Sound, New York; and Maine, where 16 were ordered for the North Haven Yacht Club in 1938, and Islesboro and Mt. Desert had fleets.

The list of owners of Herreshoff 12½s is a distinguished one. It includes such names as Forbes, Spaulding, Saltonstall, Webster, Gardner, Adams, Bourne, Belmont, Wanamaker, Honeywell, Cudahy, Tiffany, and Tillinghast.

Nathaniel Herreshoff used a hull model instead of lines drawings when designing the boat. Offsets were taken from the model and from these mold frames were constructed to shape the hull. The boat was framed in oak, and planked in cedar, upside down then turned right side up onto its keel for finishing. Eventually, due to the growing popularity of the class, three molds were necessary. The familiar oak trim was changed to mahogany in 1936.

The Herreshoff 12½ was originally a gaff-rigged sloop with self-tending jib. In 1924 Nat Herreshoff designed a Marconi rig for the boat because of the growing popularity of this type. From then on either rig was available depending on the desire of a particular fleet. For instance, in Buzzards Bay the fleets remained gaff-rigged, while in Maine, Marblehead and else-

---

Mariners Notes & Antiques, Antique Boat Society, Inc., S.W. Harbor, Manset, Me., Vol. 1, No. 4, p. 10

Dorothy I. Crossley

where the Marconi rig was popular. A wishbone boom was also designed, but never caught on. A single luff spinnaker was added quite early.

Variations were tried, but Herreshoff's original design was hard to improve upon. For example, the Fishers Island fleet, in an attempt to obtain a more seaworthy craft for the very tidal, rough water conditions there, had boats built with a wider side deck that extended across the stern. The tiller was above a lower transom. The crew had to sit further inboard, however, and the advantage of their weight balancing the boat was partly lost.

Between 1914 and 1943 Herreshoff Manufacturing Company in Bristol, Rhode Island, built about 390 Herreshoff 12½s. The first hull number was 744 and the last was 1518. The numbers in between included other kinds of Herreshoff boats as well as Herreshoff 12½s. The first boats sold for between $400 and $500, sails included, a figure that was considered high in those days!

After World War II, Cape Cod Shipbuilding Company, Wareham, Massachusetts, obtained the building works for the Herreshoff 12½ and built thirty boats in 1947–48. Quincy Adams Yacht Yard, Quincy, Massachusetts, built about twenty boats during this period using the Herreshoff mold frames. These were the last wood boats built, with the exception of a few that were privately constructed.

Nat Herreshoff did not originally give the Herreshoff 12½ a name, recording the boats as they were built simply as "12½ WL" (waterline) "M & J" (main and jib) or merely "12½." The boats were simultaneously

One of the Herreshoff 12s, called Fox Eyes, at North Haven, Maine, amidst North Haven Dinghies.

Anne White

called Buzzards Bay Class, Bristol Class, Narragansett Bay Class, and so forth, depending on where they were sailed. In Buzzards Bay, the boats carry H on the sail as a designation for H class. At North Haven, Maine, they were called Fox Eyes for the Fox Islands near which they raced. The name Bullseye has been loosely used for either the Marconi- or gaff-rigged version, but it seems to have been originally intended only for the Marconi. In 1926 the Herreshoff records show a boat listed as "Bullseye rig," distinguishing it from the next boat built which is listed as "gaff." Another popular name used for the gaff-rigged boats which sailed at the head of Buzzards Bay at Cataumet and Wings Neck was Doughdish. The story goes that Mrs. Robert Winsor's estate man was the first to use this name in about 1916. The boat's shape must have reminded him of the bowl or dish in which dough was left to rise overnight.

Today possibly 250 wood Herreshoff 12½s are still afloat. In 1948 Cape Cod Shipbuilding discontinued manufacture of wood 12s and came out with the Cape Cod Bullseye, a fiberglass boat which utilized the 12½ hull lines, but incorporated changes. The popular class, of which some 800 have been built, has a cuddy forward and a different rig.

Dorothy I. Crossley

In 1972 William Harding of Harding Sails, Marion, Massachusetts, and Peter Duff of Edey and Duff, Mattapoisett, Massachusetts, formed Doughdish, Inc. to produce a faithful fiberglass reproduction of the Herreshoff 12½. The boat, called Doughdish, is built of foam sandwich fiberglass with teak trim and is available with either gaff or Marconi rig. The H Class Association accepted it in 1973. Some seventy boats have been built so far and often race side by side with the wood 12s.

One hundred thirty-five of the 250 wood Herreshoff 12½s still afloat are in Buzzards Bay, principally sailing out of three places—Marion, Cataumet, and Quisset. Others are still active in many other areas. It is interesting to note that the 12s enjoyed such popularity that no promotion or class organization was necessary until 1972, as the number of old boats became fewer.

The Beverly Yacht Club history says that the Herreshoff 12½ was "The most popular of all classes ever raced at Beverly" and goes on to describe it as "the finest family boat ever developed, in the opinion of most of those who have sailed it." In further elaboration it is described as "a surprisingly fast little boat, quite able to take anything short of a hurricane that Buzzards Bay had to offer. It was more easily handled by a youngster than the traditional catboat, and had better sailing qualities. It could be wet, and might sink if it filled up, but that is what pumps are for, and it wouldn't capsize. Grandma could race quite comfortably in it and often did. Fathers and mothers have crewed for very small skippers, both inside and out where the wind is more apt to be."

The Herreshoff 12 is considered by many to be the best all-round sailboat of her size ever designed. Her lovely lines, seaworthiness, and fine sailing characteristics have accounted for her long-lived popularity. Her original design has remained unchanged for sixty-five years. She is a true classic.

A fiberglass Doughdish, built by Doughdish, Inc., Marion, Massachusetts.

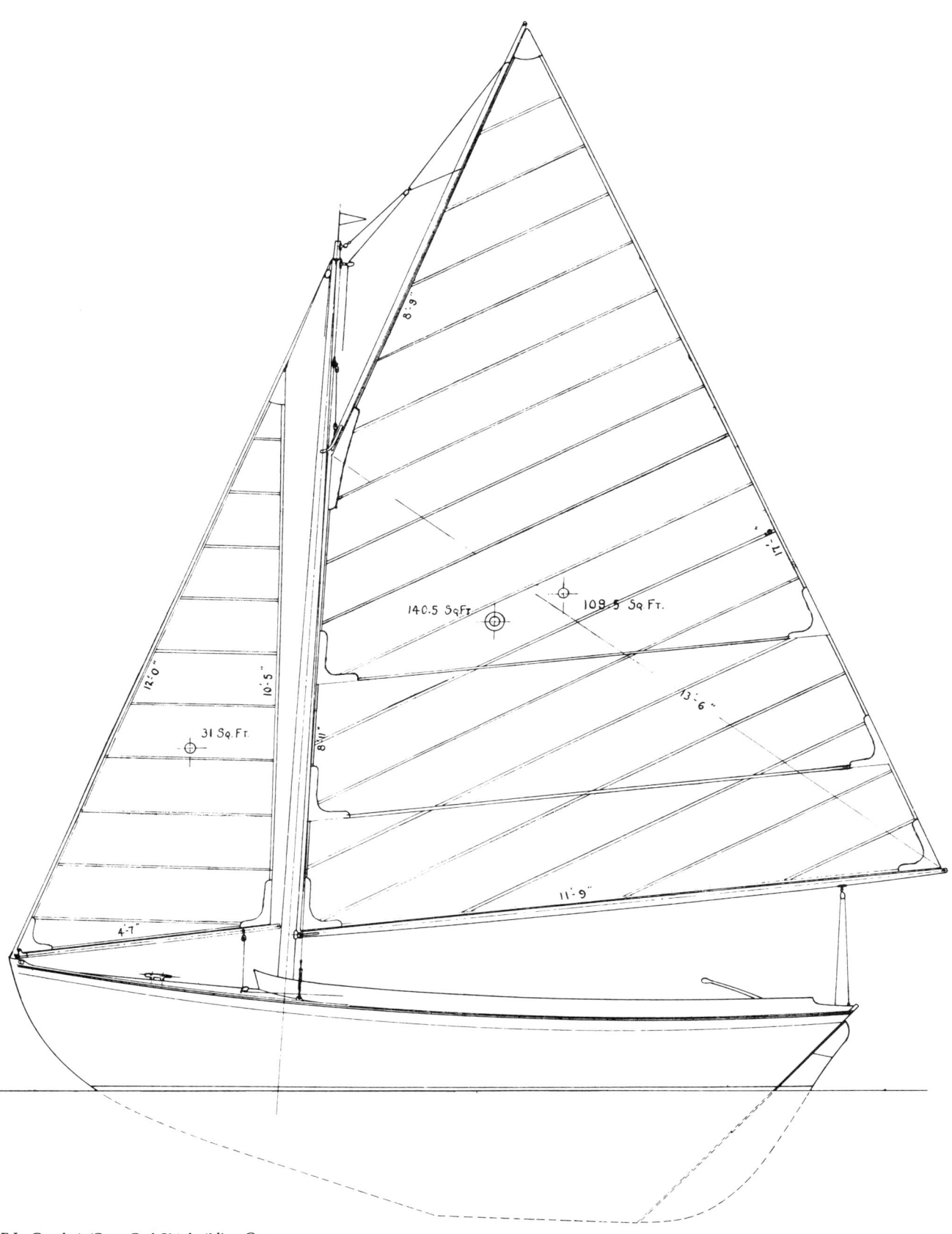

E.L. Goodwin/Cape Cod Shipbuilding Co.

The Dark Harbor 17½

(The Manchester 17½, Bar Harbor 17½ and others)

The Dark Harbor 17½ (commonly shortened to Dark Harbor 17), originally the Manchester 17½ built for the Manchester (Massachusetts) Yacht Club, continues to race at Bucks Harbor, South Brooksville, Maine, although racing has been discontinued long since in Massachusetts waters. Possibly some 200 of these beautiful gaff-rigged sloops were built, and it is not uncommon to see one or two of them in the harbors along the Maine coast. They are similar to the Northeast Harbor A boat; indeed they probably served as the inspiration for the A, which has the same waterline length of 17'6", but is 1½' longer overall. (See the Northeast Harbor A Class, page 68.)

B. B. Crowninshield designed the Manchester 17 for the Manchester Yacht Club in 1908. The design was quite successful in Manchester, Marblehead, and Cohasset, Massachusetts, and elsewhere, and attracted the attention of the sailors in Maine's wealthy coastal summer colonies. Early interest seems to have come from Islesboro, in Penobscot Bay where boats appeared at Dark Harbor's Tarratine Yacht Club and the name Dark Harbor 17 originated. Before many years elapsed fleets had been established at neighboring North Haven Island, at Northeast Harbor and Bar Harbor on Mt. Desert Island, and at Camden and Sorrento on the mainland. By the 1920s interclub regattas had begun and the fleet at Dark Harbor grew to over forty boats, necessitating dividing the class into two sections for each race. The fleet at Bucks Harbor was begun in the mid 1930s.

The boats were generally known as Manchester 17s, Dark Harbor 17s or by the place where they raced. For example, at North Haven the boats were Manchester 17s, while at Bar Harbor they were Bar Harbor 17s. At Northeast Harbor the boats were called B class to distinguish them from the Northeast Harbor A class.

After some years of active racing, new designs came along and threatened the Dark Harbor 17's popularity. The Northeast Harbor Fleet bought up the Bar Harbor boats, and the Camden Yacht Club replaced its 17s with a fleet of 32' HAJ sloops from Finland. The Dark Harbor 17 did quite well at holding her own, however. The story goes that the Camden club, soon after acquiring the Finn class sloops and intending to show them off, invited the North Haven Fleet of 17s over for a regatta. To the considerable embarrassment of the Finn sailors the Dark Harbor 17s proved to be faster and won the regatta.

The first Manchester 17s were built by the Rice Brothers Yard of East Boothbay, Maine. Later, some were built by George Lawley and Son of Neponset, Massachusetts and the Calderwood yard at Manchester, Mas-

W. H. Ballard photo

Silverwing, Northeast Harbor B Class, in 1938. Presently owned by Reverend Henry Wilder Foote, Southwest Harbor, Maine.

45

sachusetts. The last boat was built in 1935. The Dark Harbor 17 measures 25'10" overall, and 17'6" on the waterline with a beam of 6'3" and draft of 4'3". Sail area is 310 sq. ft., made up of the 245-square-foot gaff mainsail and the 65-square-foot jib. (There is also a spinnaker.) Fifteen hundred

Courtesy J. Devereux DeGozzaldi

Three 17s about to cross the finish line during a race in the late 1930s or early 40s. Note antique spinnakers.

46

lbs. of lead are carried on the oak keel. The framing is oak and the planking is white pine or cedar. There is a low trunk cabin, with 3'6" of headroom, just behind the mast, with space for two uncomfortable bunks. The original boats had a self-bailing cockpit without seats. Some boats had watertight bulkheads in the bow and stern which made them virtually unsinkable.

There have been very few changes over the years. In the 1920s the Manchester 17s switched to a Marconi rig. Most of the Maine boats continued to carry the gaff rig, however. The most notable variation was made on the Bar Harbor boats. The cabin was shortened and the self-bailing feature was removed so that the cockpit was made longer and deeper. Seats were installed. This arrangement made possible a better weight dis-

W. H. Ballard photo

Venture, Northeast Harbor B Class, in 1936.

17s racing today at Bucks Harbor.

Dark Harbor 12, a smaller Crowninshield design designed in 1915. Eleven still race at Bucks Harbor.

tribution because the crew could sit farther forward. However, the modified cabin was even more uncomfortable than the original.

Today seven or eight (of a fleet of fourteen) Dark Harbor 17s may be found racing each summer on Wednesday and Saturday afternoons at Bucks Harbor Yacht Club. (The Dark Harbor 12, a smaller Crowninshield design, also continues to race here. See Other Early One-Design Classes, page 123.) Not one of these boats is under forty-three years of age! Though they may not be quite as fast as today's modern designs with their Marconi rigs and overlapping jibs, they continue to do very well. Over the years

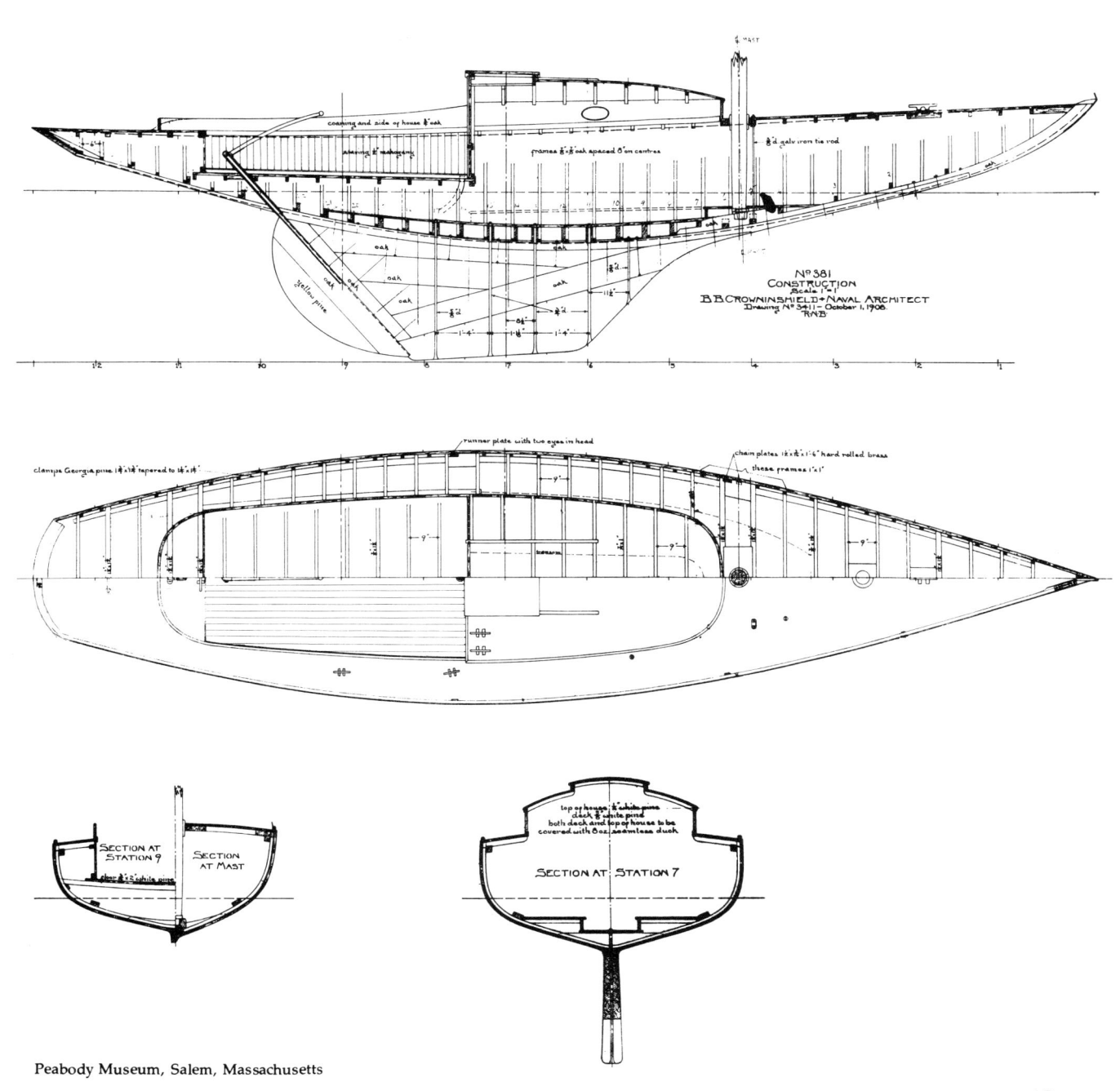

Peabody Museum, Salem, Massachusetts

they have proven to be good under all conditions. As early as the 1920s they were noted for their abilities in light air and for unusual speed reaching and before the wind. They have surely met the tests of time.

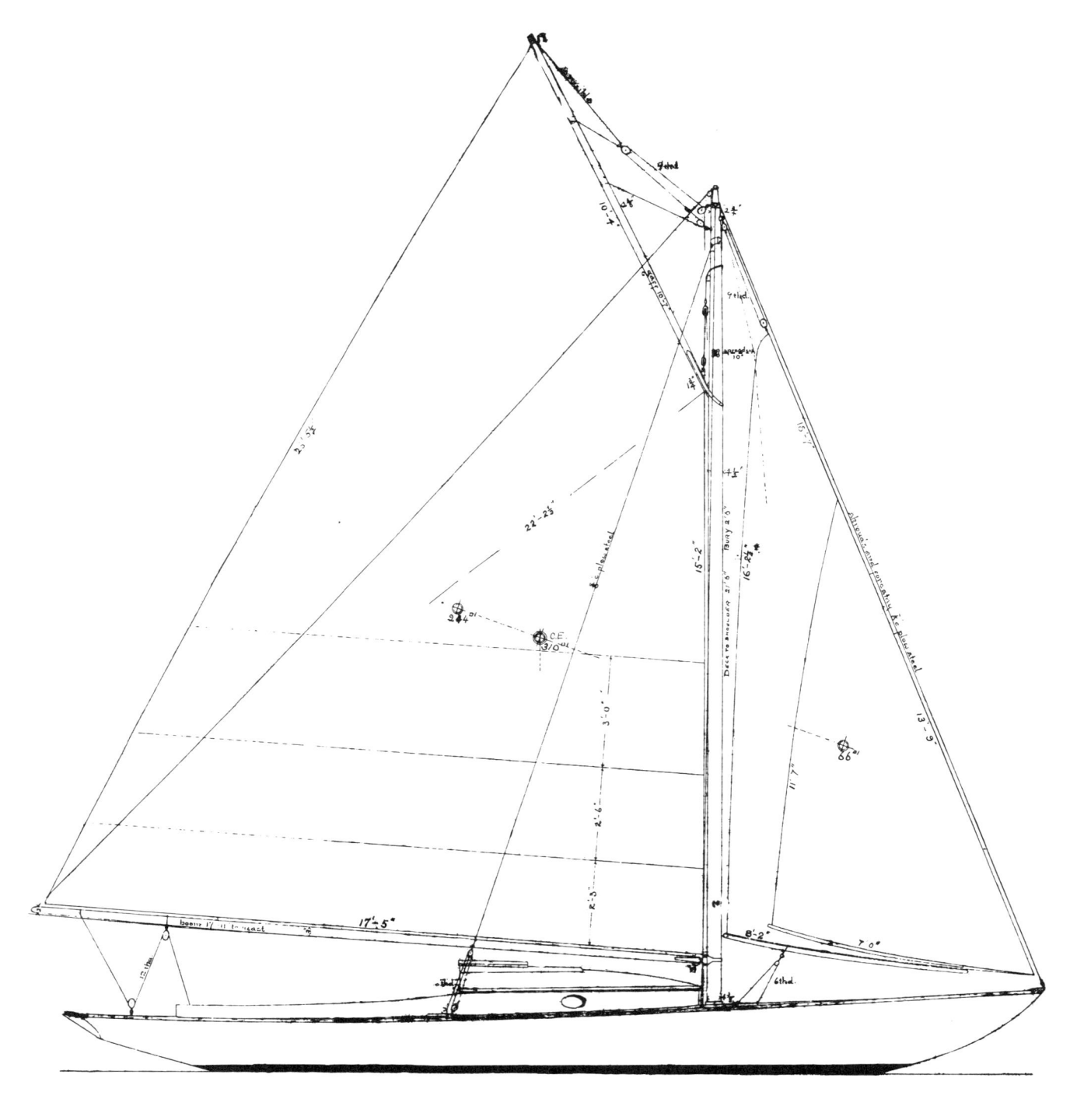

Peabody Museum, Salem, Massachusetts

The Beetle Cat

The Beetle Cat story is extraordinary. Since 1920 some 4,000 boats have been built. Today they are actively raced in forty-eight fleets. Each year 40 to 50 new wooden boats are built largely by one man, Leo Telesmanick, who has been building them for forty-eight years.

It was John Beetle of Clarks Point, New Bedford, Massachusetts, who built the first Beetle Cat Boat in 1920 for one of the children in his family. The Beetle family was noted as the builder (since 1853) of the famous Beetle Whaleboat, the boat which was lowered away at the sighting of a whale and from which the harpooning took place. Needless to say, the Beetle family was known for its ability to build fine, strong boats.

The Beetle Cat design was based on that of the Cape Cod Catboat, a stable fishing craft designed to work the shallows along Cape Cod and survive in rough water. As with any of the more successful one-designs, it has features and qualities eminently suited to the locale in which it is sailed and to the people who sail it. A centerboard boat, it has a rudder that doesn't extend below the skeg, so when the centerboard is pulled up it can skim over the numerous shoals. It has a great beam of 6', nearly half its length of 12'4", which makes it very stable, almost impossible to capsize. Its single gaff-rigged mainsail causes the boat to head up into the wind when the tiller is released, and it can be reefed without losing the proper center of effort. Made of wood with no ballast, it is virtually unsinkable. For these reasons it is an excellent children's boat. Weighing only 450 lbs., it is trailerable and it can be beached for a picnic. The large cockpit, well aft, provides space for as many as four and leaves a large deck area forward to catch the spray.

John Beetle's new catboat was quick to draw attention, and he began to manufacture the boats using mass production methods that his brother Charles employed in building whaleboats. This kept the cost within the means of the not-so-rich. (The boat originally sold for $250.) As early as 1923 there was a fleet in Duxbury, Massachusetts. By the late 1920s and early 1930s Beetle Cat fleets had sprung up on Cape Cod at such places as Barnstable and Bass River, and on Buzzards and Narragansett Bays.

When John died in 1928 his daughter, Ruth Beetle, took over the business. It was claimed that she was the only woman boatwright in the country at the time. Ruth's semiretired uncle, Charles Beetle, and his son-in-law, John Baumann, ran the shop. In 1930, at the age of fifteen, Leo Telesmanick went to work for them as a three-year apprentice and then as a three-year journeyman. He started out chopping wood and firing the steam boiler, but went on to learn all phases of building the Beetle Cats. Mr. Beetle and Mr. Baumann taught him how to select the lumber and put it to good use, and even sent him to evening school to study machine shop practices and mechanical drawing. In 1936, upon the death of John

Photo by Norman Fortier

Baumann, Ruth Beetle put Leo in charge of production and, except for the war years, he has been building Beetles ever since.

Building at Clarks Point stopped in 1941, and during World War II Leo went to work for Palmer Scott Company building boats for the army and navy. In 1946 Ruth Beetle and her brother, Carl, who had become involved in the company and was interested in building fiberglass boats, sold the Beetle Company to Waldo Howland of Concordia Company, builders of the lovely Concordia Yawl. It was arranged for Leo Telesmanick, still with Palmer Scott Company, to build the Beetle Cat for Concordia. This arrangement ended in 1960 when the Beetle Cat operation, and Leo with it, moved to Smith Neck, South Dartmouth, Massachusetts, where the Beetles have been built since. In August, 1969 Waldo and Louie Howland, sole owners of Concordia Co., Inc., sold the business to the current owner, William Pinney, Jr.

Photo by Norman Fortier

Photo by Norman Fortier

Little has changed from the first Beetle to the latest. Modern tools are used and the boats are built upside down now instead of right side up as they were at first. The fastenings have changed from galvanized to bronze. The running rigging is Dacron or nylon because high-grade manila is no longer available. The boats are still framed in white oak, which is obtained locally, and planked in cedar. The deck is painted canvas, and the handsome cockpit coaming is varnished steam-bent oak. The spar stock is Douglas Fir. Of course the price has changed, but it is quite surprising to discover that the Beetle Cat sells for around $1,800 less sail, considerably less than fiberglass boats of its size.

At any time you can find Leo Telesmanick and three or four others at work in the Smith Neck shop building Beetles, five at a time, to the same high standards as in the early days.

Today the Beetle Cats race in thirty-three New England Beetle Catboat Association fleets, primarily on the Massachusetts South Shore, Cape Cod, Buzzards Bay, Narragansett Bay and the Connecticut shore. Another fifteen nonmember fleets sail in these same waters as well as on Long Island's Great South Bay. In addition, individual Beetle Cats may be found most anyplace—in Colorado, on the West Coast, the British Virgin Islands, Florida, Texas and Hawaii, to name a few. In 1971, William Pinney donated a new Beetle Cat to Mystic Seaport. The New England Beetle Catboat Association was formed in 1937 with the following clubs as charter members: Angelica (Mattapoisett), Barnstable, Bass River, and New Bedford, all in Massachusetts, and Barrington and Edgewood, in Rhode Island. Five championships are held each summer: Mitey Mite (for youngsters under twelve years of age), Juniors, Men, Women, and Tired Parents (parent as skipper, with children or grandchildren as crew).

Leo Telesmanick says that Charles Beetle told him, "As long as people continue to get married and have children Beetles will be built and sailed." Leo himself says, "When a man buys a Beetle he does not usually give

Leo Telesmanick and a Beetle Cat in the Smith Neck Shop.

much thought to its design or construction. It is only after he has watched the boat being handed down from one child to another that he begins to realize there is something unusual about his boat"—something special.

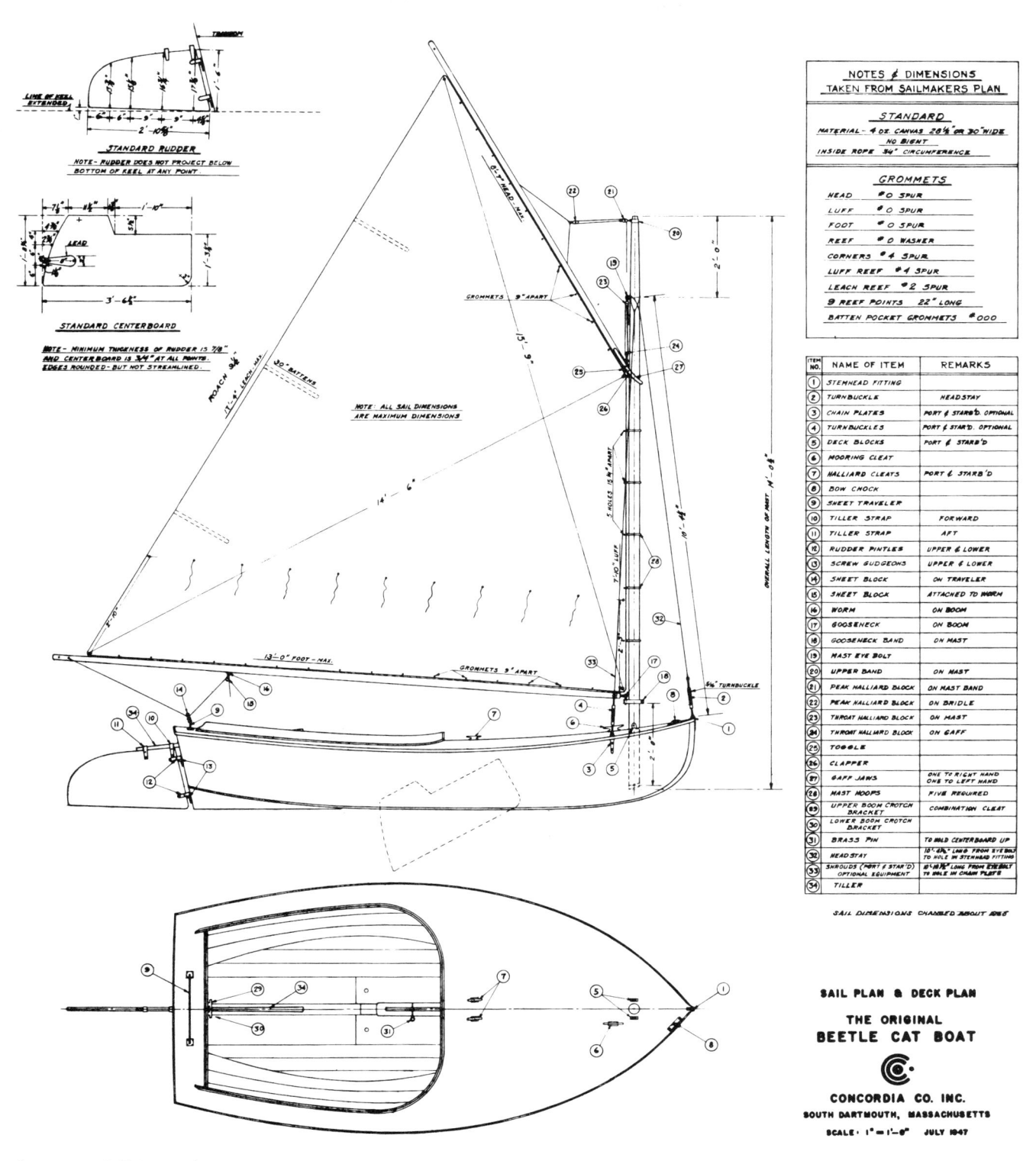

Courtesy Leo J. Telesmanick, Manager, Beetle Cat Division, Concordia Co., Inc.

The Idem

The Idem is incomparable. Not only is it among the very oldest one-designs still actively racing (built in 1900 and 1902), but it is the *original* boats that are still competing. Today, eight out of a total of twelve that were built still race on Upper St. Regis Lake in the Adirondack Mountains of New York. Ten of the original twelve are still registered with the St. Regis Yacht Club. The Idem is almost certainly the oldest actively racing one-design class consisting of only original boats.

Idem means *the same* or *identical* in Latin. It was because the summer campers at Upper St. Regis and adjoining Spitfire Lakes, who had formed a yacht club in 1898, wanted a class of boats to race that were all alike that the Idem came into existence.

In 1897 Augustus Durkee, one of the founders of the St. Regis Yacht Club, brought *Momo,* one of the American challengers for the Seawanhaka Cup, to Upper St. Regis Lake. *Momo* was designed and raced by the well-known naval architect, Clinton Crane. Crane unsuccessfully designed and sailed several contenders for the Cup after losing it to the Royal St. Lawrence Yacht Club of Montreal in 1896. Regardless of the effectiveness of his Seawanhaka designs in Canada, the sailors on Upper St. Regis Lake were impressed when *Momo,* with Crane at the helm, beat all comers. In 1899 Crane was contracted to design the Idem over the winter of 1899–1900. Seven were built for the 1900 summer season by the Spaulding–St. Lawrence Boat Company of Ogdensburg, New York. These were numbers 20 through 26, *Shadow, Maita, Kingfisher, Flying Fretz, Water Witch, Elfmere,* and *Peekaboo.* An additional five (numbers 27 through 31, *Sure Mike, Eadem, Pulpit Rocket, Nameless,* and *Water Sprite*) were built in 1902. The cost for each boat was $750.

Before Crane began designing the Idem he studied the wind conditions on Upper St. Regis Lake. He apparently noted the extremes of wind velocity which can be present on any given day. Because of high land near shore there are always spots where there is little wind even on very windy days. Crane took this into account in his design. The Idem, with its large sail area, is responsive and can take advantage of light airs. When it blows hard the boat will heel over and spill the wind but remain stable because of its beam and heavy centerboard.

Crane's Idem design was an example of the faster designs created by use of the waterline length plus sail area rule of the time (length plus square root of sail area divided by 2). With a short waterline length, and long overhang, large sail areas could be used. This was found to give maximum speed. It is interesting to note that it was probably because

John B. Trevor, Jr. photo

Crane's designs were not as extreme as those of his competitors in this regard that he was defeated in some of the Seawanhaka Cup Races. These same boats which beat Crane, in particular the *Dominion*, influenced the evolution of the Inland Lake Scows.

The Idem is a gaff-rigged sloop which measures 32' overall, and 19' on the waterline, with an 8' beam and 23" draft with centerboard up. The hull draft is actually only 10½", but there are 600 to 700 lbs. of lead in the weighted centerboard which cannot be withdrawn up into the trunk and thus create the additional draft. The boat displaces between 6,500 and 6,800 lbs. The sail area is 600 sq. ft., comprised of main and jib. A spinnaker is additional. The Idem keel and framing is white oak and the carvel planking is cedar with white oak sheer strake. Fastenings are copper and bronze. The deck is canvas over pine or cedar. Trim is mahogany. Most hulls are varnished. There is no external keel.

One may well wonder how it is that the Idem has survived so well structurally for so long. One reason is superb craftsmanship. In addition, a key is that the hull is strengthened by two trusses which run lengthwise inside the hull just outside either side of the cockpit. These trusses are made up of two longitudinal stringers, one running across the frames and the other along under the deck. The stringers are connected by crisscrossed pieces bolted to the stringers and to each other in the middle. This provides a lightweight structural support for the hull.

The Idem has held her own through the years against the influx of other sailboat designs on Upper St. Regis Lake. Even E Scows were generally beaten except under very strong wind conditions. Interestingly, the Idem has outlasted her fastest competitor, the Raven, which came along in the 1950s and could consistently beat her.

John B. Trevor, Jr. photo

In spite of her success, ideas for improving the Idem have been entertained. Though her owners sometimes deny it, she has her faults. When heeled way over, her centerboard and rudder are out of the water and she can't be controlled. It has been suggested that she should have double rudders and bilgeboards. Most Idem owners are resistent to change, but not all. One went so far as to retain a naval architect to design a Marconi rig for his Idem. The change turned out to be a complicated one. A much taller mast than the 30' original was required. The lead weight on the centerboard had to be doubled, and winches and other rig changes were required. The result was a disaster. The Marconi-rigged Idem could not even keep up with her gaff-rigged sisters, let alone beat them. In addition, she began to leak badly. It was eventually discovered that the additional weight on her centerboard had caused the centerboard trunk fastenings to shear. And so she has been returned to her original gaff-rigged state.

The Idem celebrated her seventy-fifth anniversary in 1975 with a two-day regatta consisting of five races. Six boats competed and the scoring was amazingly close, with five different boats taking first place in each of the five races. Today, nine of the original twelve Idems are still sailable, or potentially so, on Upper St. Regis Lake. Two others have been sold off the lake, but are still active. The twelfth, *Water Witch* was donated to the Adirondack Museum and is beautifully displayed, fully rigged with sails up, afloat under a glass dome.

Clinton Crane, in his autobiography (1952), commented on the longevity of his Idem design and went on to say "I made up my mind then, and I have not changed it since, that a one-design class, to be a success, must be relatively fast as compared to other boats of similar size and must be fun to sail." He surely had the key. What a success his Idem has been!

John B. Trevor, Jr. photo

John B. Trevor, Jr. photo

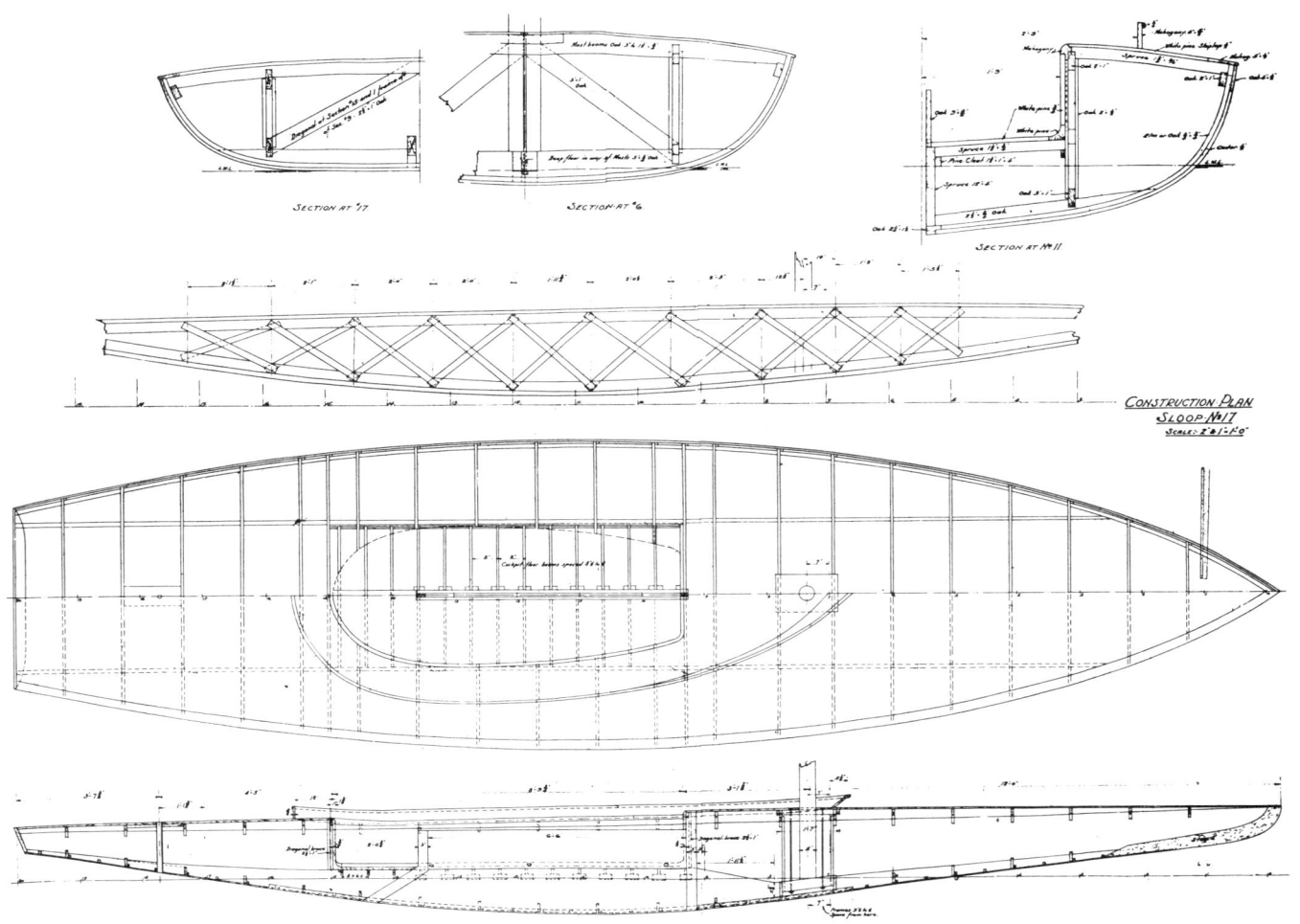

The Adirondack Museum, Blue Mountain Lake, N.Y.

The 18' (Cape Cod Baby) Knockabout

The 18' (Cape Cod Baby) Knockabout has been built in greater numbers than any other one-design of its size designed before 1925, with the exception of the Star. Nearly 3,000 wood hulls were built before fiberglass was accepted for construction in 1960. Since then 115 fiberglass Knockabouts have been built. The history of the class is one of change and evolution. As with the Star, only the hull has remained unchanged since conception. It is because of the Knockabout's versatility, together with her hull design, which is well suited to the waters in which she sails, and the enthusiasm and persistence of her skippers, that the class has survived impressively when threatened with extinction. Today the class is the strongest of its type on Massachusetts's Cape Cod.

Captain Charles Guerney designed and built the first Cape Cod Baby Knockabouts in 1918. Guerney was not a sea captain or even a seagoing man, but he nevertheless designed many fine power and sailing craft. He and his brother, Myron, both of whom were experienced wheelwrights, opened a shop on Main St. in Wareham, Massachusetts in the early 1900s. Curiously, they soon went into the business of building dories for fishing and pleasure. They named their business Cape Cod Power Dory Company, and Myron became shop foreman, while Charles was designer and salesman. About 1911, Captain Guerney built a small sloop which was probably the prototype of the 1918 Knockabout. By 1921, with the investment of outside capital, the business had become Cape Cod Shipbuilding Company, and had moved to Narrows Rd., Wareham. Building of 18' Knockabouts and other craft began in earnest. The boat became popular fast, and by the mid-twenties enough had been built so that they were raced in southern Massachusetts waters.

The first Cape Cod Baby Knockabouts were inexpensive, costing around $175 including a "sail away lunch," and advertised as the "poor man's yacht." The specifications were 18' overall, and 15'9" on the waterline, with a draft of 14" with centerboard up and 4'2" with board down. The boats were framed in white oak and planked in white cedar. Guerney's hull design was an excellent solution to the problems presented by the shallow waters and choppy conditions of Buzzards Bay. The rounded bilges took the seas well, and the deep forefoot cut through the chop to minimize pounding. The centerboard could be raised to skim over the shoals. The hull went well to windward and was stable before the wind. It is no wonder the design has survived unchanged to this day.

Guerney's rig was less successful. Because the boat was to be used by children, he designed a low-aspect-ratio rig (less than 1½ to 1) with a small jib and oversized main, combined with a small rudder. This produced a heavy-weather helm so that when the wind blew much over twelve knots the boat would head safely into the wind. The boat was very difficult to handle when the wind piped up. It wasn't long before some of the experienced sailors who got ahold of her started to make changes, a practice which has continued to this day. Bigger jibs and smaller mains were used. The rig became higher in aspect. Deeper rudders and larger centerboards were incorporated. Cape Cod Shipbuilding Company adopted most of the early changes which improved the Knockabout's sailing characteristics.

The Cape Cod Baby Knockabout's popularity became far-ranging. In the 1930s, a fleet of over 100 raced on Long Island, New York's, Great South Bay. There were also fleets in Maine, Narragansett Bay, Rhode Island, New Jersey, eastern Connecticut, on the Great Lakes and elsewhere. It was on the south side of Massachusetts's Cape Cod that the class attained its most long-lived popularity, however.

By 1930 some of the Southern Massachusetts Yacht Racing Association clubs were racing Cape Cod Baby Knockabouts and there was some interclub activity. About this time the Knockabouts were first started as a class in the Edgartown Regatta. In 1934 the fleets at Lewis Bay, Woods Hole, Waquoit, Bass River, Vineyard Haven, and Menauhant formed the Cape Cod Knockabout Class Association, and held the first annual regatta on August 11, 1934. This competition brought a flurry of redesigning to make win-producing improvements within the specifications. The enthusiasm spread to Chapoquoit and Wenaumet Bluffs Clubs, which joined the organization by 1938, bringing the total membership to eight. In this year spinnakers were first allowed in regatta racing. In 1940 sixty-seven Knockabouts were entered in the annual regatta, a high point for the class.

Preregatta races, which were long-distance races to the site of the regatta, had begun in the late thirties, and proved quite challenging. The 1941 race from Hyannis to Woods Hole, a distance of about twenty-five miles in a straight line, was sailed entirely against a head wind and tide with boats finishing around 9 P.M.

Regattas were terminated with the outbreak of World War II. After the war, they were resumed, with fifty-one boats entering the first held at Waquoit in 1946. The fleets at Lewis Bay, Chapoquoit, and Wenaumet Bluffs were not reinstated, but a new fleet was formed at Megansett. The Cape Cod Shipbuilding Company Trophy was introduced to be awarded to the skipper who scored the most points for his or her club in the annual regatta. 1950 was one of the high points of postwar activity. In addition to a season of very competitive racing, it brought total revision of the class specifications.

The fifties brought a series of misfortunes and problems for the class which nearly brought about its extinction. The Korean War took many sailors into the armed services. Next, Cape Cod Shipbuilding Company discontinued construction of the Knockabouts. No sooner had this decision occurred than Hurricane Carol came along and destroyed or damaged nearly half of the existing boats. Through considerable dedicated effort, the boats were rebuilt or replaced with other secondhand boats so that the class might continue to race. It was apparent, however, that a new source of Knockabouts must be found.

In 1958 Bruce Barnard built a wood prototype hull from the plans Robert Stanton Fox had drawn up based on Prince Crowell's *Imp*. In 1959 Frost took over the complete building of fiberglass Knockabouts and the first of these competed that year. In 1964, after forty-six fiberglass hulls

Wood Knockabout *Nike*.

Dorothy I. Crossley

had been built, Bruce Barnard sold the molds to the 18' Knockabout Class Association. The Association now licenses boat builders to construct the custom fiberglass boats. Construction has averaged four or five boats per year over the past fourteen years. Finest quality materials are used, including matched teak for coaming and cedar or redwood for floorboards. In 1975, a new hull and deck mold was built. The current active builder is master craftsman Damian McLaughlin of North Falmouth, Massachusetts. The price at this writing is about $4,500.

Fiberglass Knockabout *John Galt*. ▶

1954 Knockabout race at Woods Hole. Note single luff spinnakers.

Dorothy I. Crossley

Dorothy I. Crossley

Except for her hull, the 18' Knockabout of today is very different from the Cape Cod Baby Knockabout of the 1920s. Innovation and change have been part of the fun for the Knockabout sailor, and the "improvements" have been endless. Besides rudder, centerboard, jib, and aspect-ratio changes, sails have been completely redesigned, spreaders have been replaced with double shrouds, a spinnaker has been added and changed three times—everything from the ballast to the battens has been altered. One-design specifications have become more strict with the years, but even today only the hull is off limits. Changes are permitted to centerboard, rig and rudder, within certain specified boundaries.

Today forty to sixty boats participate in regattas, which include a National Championship and the SMYRA Championship, the forty-first of which was held in 1978. Fleets are active at Megansett, Woods Hole, Waquoit, Hyannis, Lewis Bay, Bass River, and West Dennis, Massachusetts. A few wood boats, beautifully maintained, participate in the regattas. Smaller fleets are still active in Rhode Island and on Lake Champlain, and individual boats may be found all over.

With her modern rig, newly designed rudder and centerboard, rachet blocks, and contemporary fittings, the 18' Knockabout is a joy to sail. Requiring only a light two-finger touch to control her helm, she will climb to weather through the worst chop. Today the class has as many, if not more, dedicated sailors than ever before, and it is easy to understand why.

Courtesy 18' Knockabout Class Association

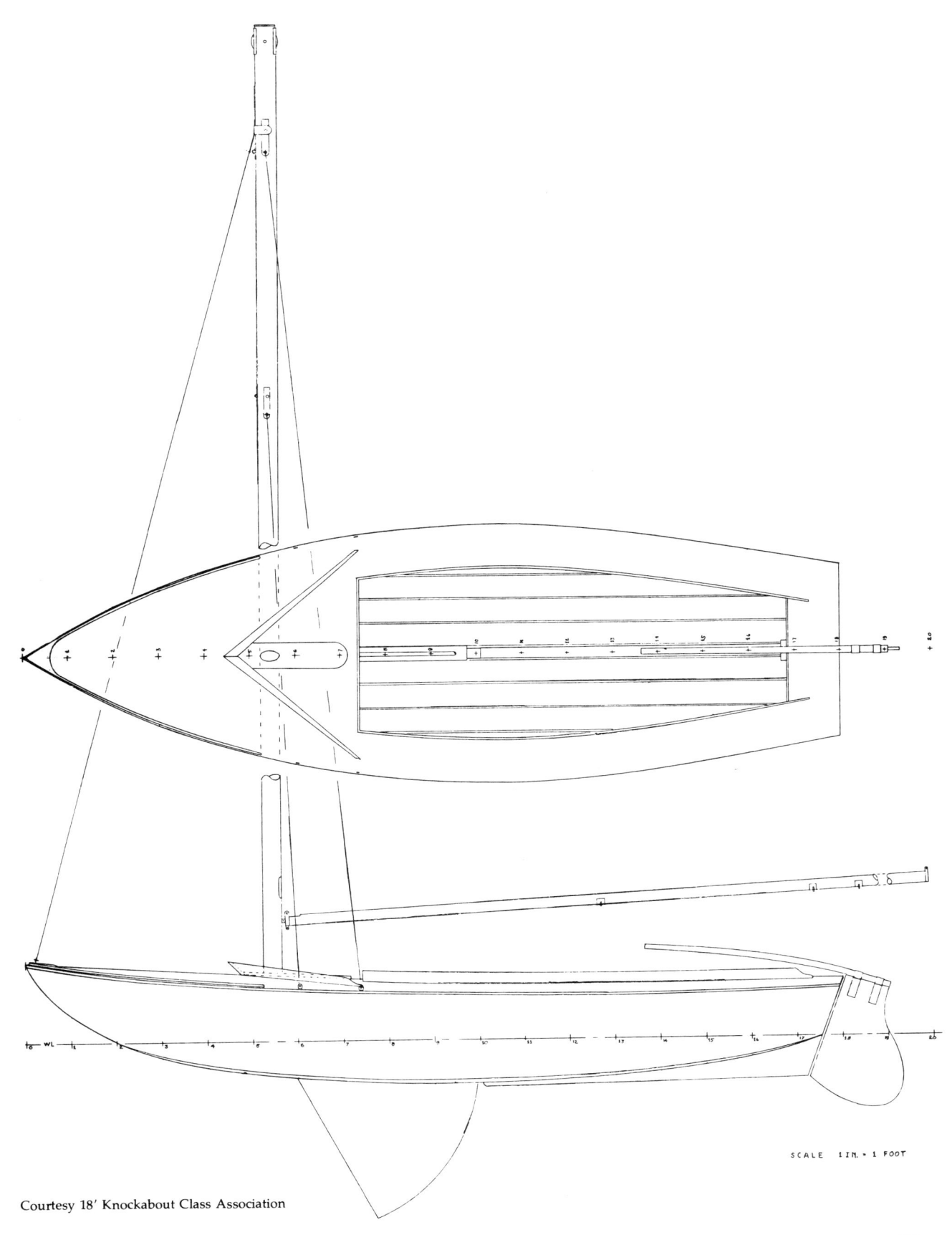

SCALE 1 IN. = 1 FOOT

67

The Northeast Harbor A
(Eastern Yacht Club 17' Gaff-rigged Sloop Knockabout Class)

Like her slightly older, smaller, similar sister, the Dark Harbor 17½ (originally the Manchester 17), the Northeast Harbor A was born in Massachusetts and moved to Maine. No doubt Herbert M. Sears, vice commodore and later commodore of the Eastern Yacht Club, Marblehead, Massachusetts (who founded the Sears Cup National Juniors Championship annual competition), along with fellow members, saw the Manchester 17½ and determined to have a similar boat designed. Consequently, Edwin A. Boardman was commissioned in 1911 to design a similar, slightly larger, but less expensive boat—a difficult task! The Eastern Yacht Club 17' Gaff-rigged Sloop Knockabout which Boardman came up with had nearly the same waterline length as the Manchester 17½ (17'), but was more than 1½' longer overall (27'6" as compared with 25'10"). Other design specifications were 7'3" beam, 4' draft, and 368 sq. ft. of sail area. It had a watertight, self-bailing cockpit. The boat was framed in white oak, planked with cypress, and fastened with copper rivets. The Swedish-steel, bolted-on fin keel was the economic concession which made the boat less expensive than the Dark Harbor 17½, which had a wineglass-shaped keel.

Twenty-five of these boats were built for the 1912 season by George Lawley and Son of Neponset, Massachusetts (a renowned builder of quality yachts) at a cost of between $500 and $700 apiece. Known by a variety of names including EYC 17 Footers, Marblehead One-designs, EYC One-designs, and Marblehead 17s, they raced at Marblehead in 1912 and 1913. Something of a toy, the boats were often slung on davits and carried on the palatial yachts of their wealthy owners. Apparently, after the 1913 season the Eastern Yacht Club members tired of them and decided to try a new design. Several boats, including Herbert M. Sears's number 1, *Daffydill*, were put up for sale. Six boats were bought for the 1914 season by the wealthy summer residents of Northeast Harbor on Maine's beautiful Mt. Desert Island. Henry Parkman bought *Daffydill*; Edward W. Madeira and Francis C. Grant in partnership, number 2, *Ino*; Ernest B. Dane, Jr., number 4, *Atlanta*; William S. Grant, Jr., number 7, *Moslem III*; W.W. Rowse, number 14, *Squaw*; and Dr. Richard H. Harte, number 17, *Kipper*.

Racing was interrupted by World War I, but resumed afterwards and the class became ever more popular. Eventually all the Marblehead boats were purchased by Northeast Harbor summer residents. At first the racing was very informal, with government buoys or islands as marks and someone standing up in a rowboat to call the start.

In 1921 the boats acquired the name Northeast Harbor A Class of the Northeast Harbor Fleet. The B Class was the Dark Harbor 17½ (formerly the Manchester 17½). The Fleet became a yacht club in 1923. In 1926, with the A Class so popular that a good boat was selling for as much as $1,500,

Antique Boat Society, Inc. Archives, Manset, Maine/W. H. Ballard photo

it was decided that more boats were needed. Rice Brothers in East Boothbay, Maine was contracted to build twenty-five additional sloops from the original plans. With the addition of the new yachts, some forty to forty-five boats were at the starting line for each race. The resulting melee made it obvious that two divisions with separate starts were necessary. At first, division was determined by drawing lots, but eventually it became apparent that the older Lawley boats were somewhat faster than the new Rice boats and this determined grouping. The Rice Brothers boats were wider in the stern than the original Lawley boats. How this occurred has caused speculation. Robert Rice says his grandfather, the builder, was instructed by a Northeast Harbor Yacht Club representative to alter the plans so that the boats would be more stable and drier.

For ten years or more forty to forty-five boats started each race. Gradually, from the late 1930s on, newer designs, first the International One Designs and later the Luders 16s, with modern Marconi rigs without run-

Antique Boat Society, Inc. Archives, Manset, Maine/W. H. Ballard photo

Antique Boat Society, Inc. Archives, Manset, Maine/W. H. Ballard photo/reprinted with permission from *Down East* Magazine, Camden, Maine

A's race in the Western Way off Northeast Harbor.

ning backstays, began intruding on the boats' popularity. The two divisions became one again, but on a weekly basis competition extended into the sixties, when it was reduced to an annual regatta. A proposal to change the rig from gaff to Marconi was considered at one time, but it was never implemented. In 1961 a fiftieth anniversary regatta was held with *Daffydill*, skippered by Henry Flagler Harris, winning. Thirteen others, including *Ino* and *Kipper*, raced off Mt. Desert Island. The last annual regatta took place in 1971 under the auspices of the Oceanus Dolphins Club. Each year the Antique Boat Society sponsors a race in which a few Northeast Harbor As as well as other antique boats race.

Posterity for the class was insured in 1975 with the donation of A number 7 to Mystic Seaport Museum, but better still, perhaps half the original fifty boats are still afloat. Ten or so are in local waters and the rest are interspersed along the East Coast from Maine to Maryland. Number 50, *Gull*, still owned by the son of her original owner, Sunoco oil heir and executive R. Anderson Pew, remains a well-maintained example of this fine class.

Antique Boat Society, Inc. Archives, Manset, Maine/W.H. Ballard photo/reprinted with permission from *Down East* Magazine, Camden, Maine

Robert B. Rice collection

The second lot of A Boats being built at Rice Brothers, April, 1927.

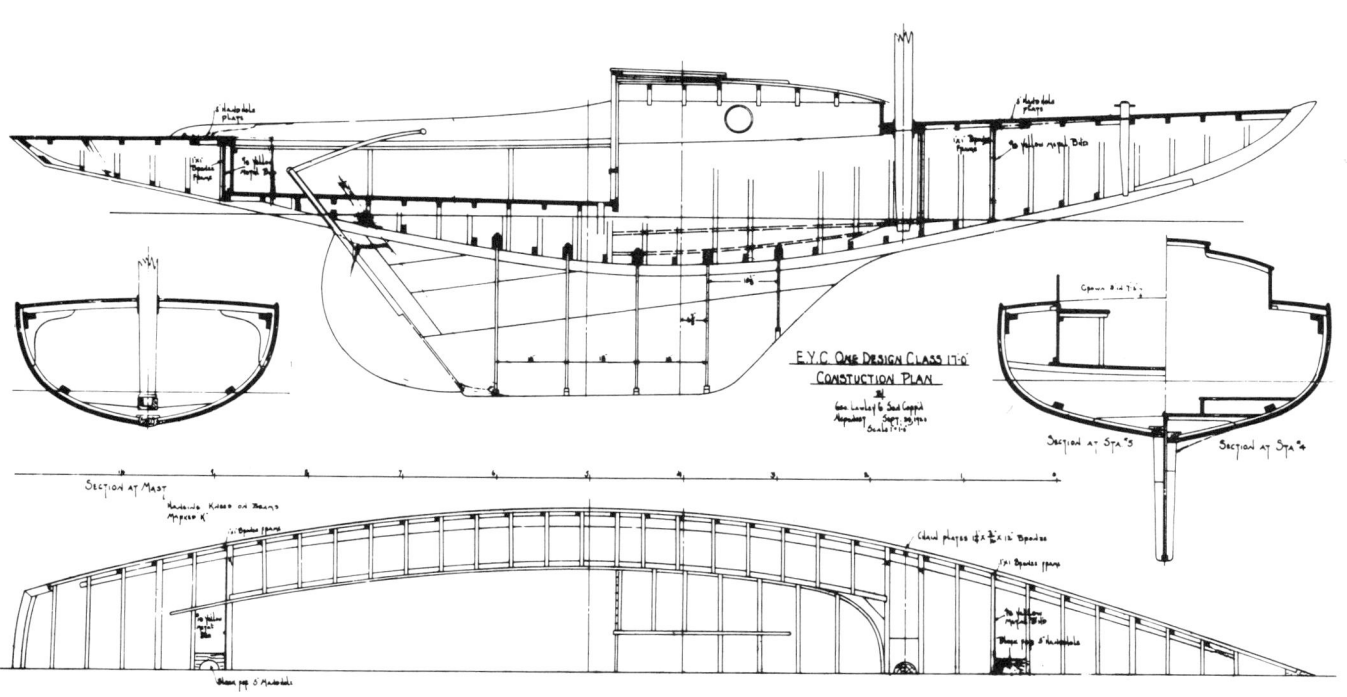

Hart Nautical Museum, M.I.T.

73

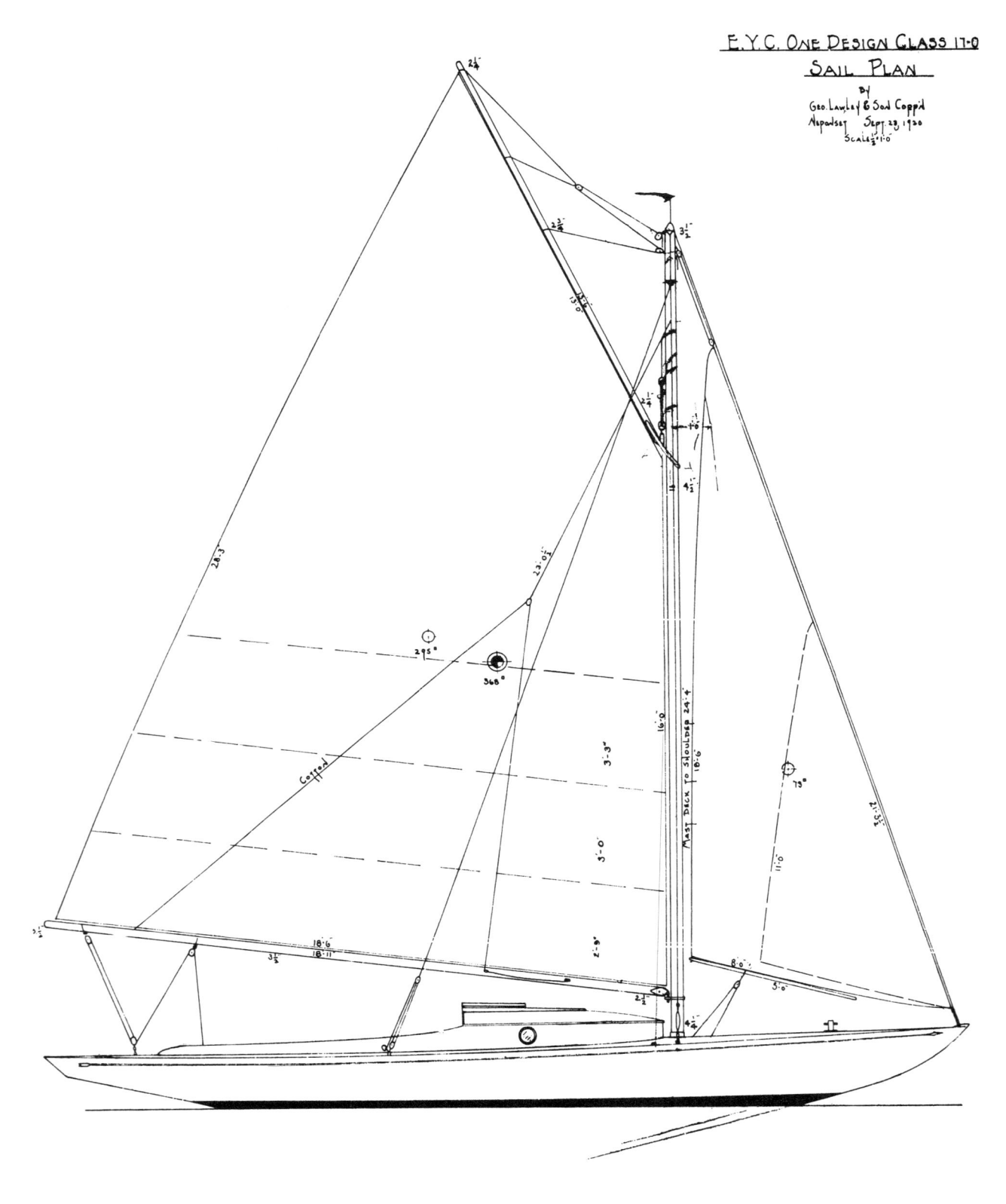

The SS

One of the oldest active one-designs, the SS is an attractive, little-known boat that races at the eastern end of Long Island's South Shore. First raced in 1909, this 16' gaff-rigged, centerboard sloop seems to have survived the inroads made by more modern designs very nicely. Today about thirty still sail and race on Moriches and Shinnecock Bays.

In 1908 William C. Atwater (who became commodore of the Westhampton Yacht Squadron in 1912) asked Benjamin Hallock of Center Moriches, New York to design and build a sloop of 16', with mainsail, club jib and no ballast. Hallock had been a student of Gil Smith, the noted Long Island catboat builder, and the longevity of the design he came up with indicates he knew his business. Nine boats were built for the 1909 season. These were numbered 11–20 (omitting 13) to give the impression that there were more than nine boats on the Bay. Sails were designed by Hallock, and Everett Benjamin. These first boats sold for the amazing price of $125, sails included.

Hallock built the boats from a half model scaled one inch to the foot. When he died in 1931 and measurements for plans were taken off several of his boats it was interesting to note that none of the dimensions varied more than an inch and a half. The boats were framed out of hackmatack knees which were sawn to shape, planked and decked in cedar, and the keel, deck beams and coaming were cypress. The spars were fir or white pine. The SS dimensions were 16'5⅝" overall, 14' on the waterline, beam of 4'9" and draft of 15" with the board up and 33" with the board down. Sail area was approximately 133 sq. ft., comprising 100 sq. ft. of mainsail and 33 sq. ft. of jib.

Hallock went on to build boats 1–10 in 1914 and another twenty boats (40–59) in 1924. From then on till his death he built forty-four boats (60–103). Sam Newey built hull numbers 21–39 between 1921 and 1928. Although he was a successful boatbuilder, his SSs turned out to be inferior to Hallock's. They were therefore given a Marconi rig and raced separately as the M class, beginning in 1924. After Hallock's death, Oliver Howell became the official builder and built about twenty-five boats between 1931 and 1941. Howard Welsh, of Nickerson Boat Yard, East Moriches, followed him, building about twenty boats. Louis Howell (no relation to Oliver and not an official builder) built three or four boats. Fred Scopinich built the latest SS, number 154, in 1968.

The newest SS is very similar to the oldest. The original club jib was replaced by a free-footed jib quite early. A reaching spinnaker was added in the 1930s and replaced in 1969 by a balloon spinnaker. The sail material for main and jib has changed of course, from the original duck, to canvas, to Egyptian cotton, and now Dacron. After World War II it became impossible to obtain hackmatack knees to frame the SS. Production was temporarily halted, but was resumed when the SS Association permitted the use of molded plywood ribs. SSs 148–154 were built with plywood in the 1960s. Some of the hulls have been fiberglassed for preservation.

The meaning of Hallock's designation, SS, has been lost in time. Apparently no one thought to ask what it stood for, or at least record the meaning. SS may have stood for Special Sloop, or Small Sloop, or even South Shore. Or perhaps the boat was thus distinguished from the popular Herreshoff S.

The SS is exciting and challenging to race. There is always wind and sea in Moriches and Shinnecock Bays. The boats are fast, and because of their low freeboard, they will swamp. The crew generally gets drenched. Each boat has its own well-worn bailing scoop. If it goes overboard it is practically a necessity to go back and pick it up in order to finish the race. In addition, the boats are tricky because they tend to nose dive. They come up, if the skipper heads up, but you don't win races that way!

The SS has been the inspiration for two other classes. The Moriches Bay One Design was designed in 1928 by Benjamin Hallock and, at 24'9", was essentially a larger, more comfortable SS that could be day sailed as well as raced. The Cottontail is a contemporary, Marconi-rigged, fiberglass racing sloop. Based on the SS, the hull has more freeboard and a reverse transom.

SS Class race about 1925.

Morris Rosenfeld photo

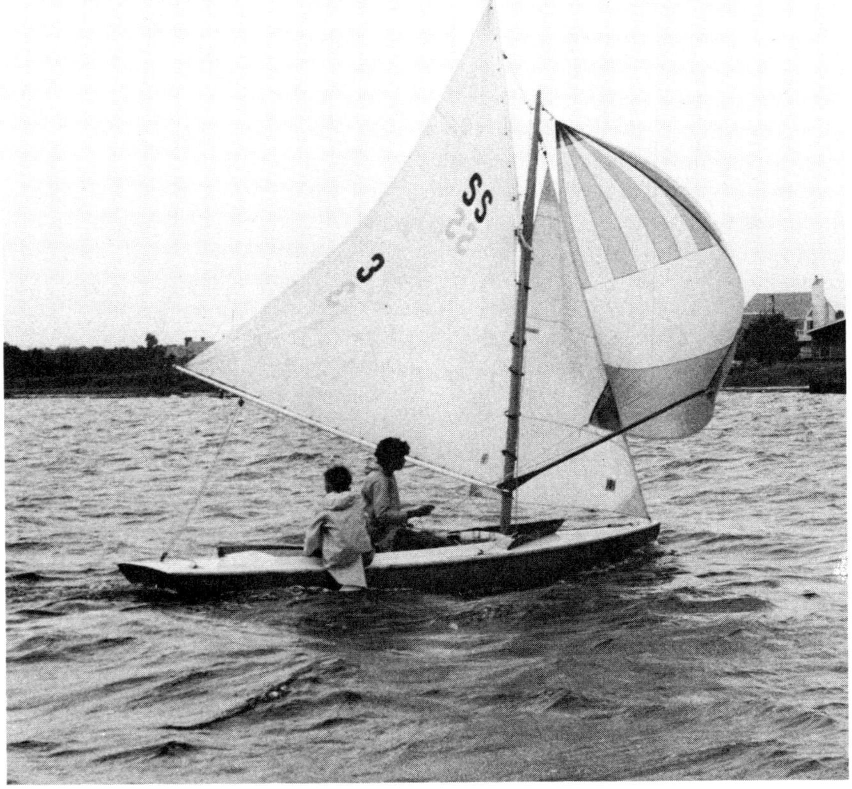
SS
3

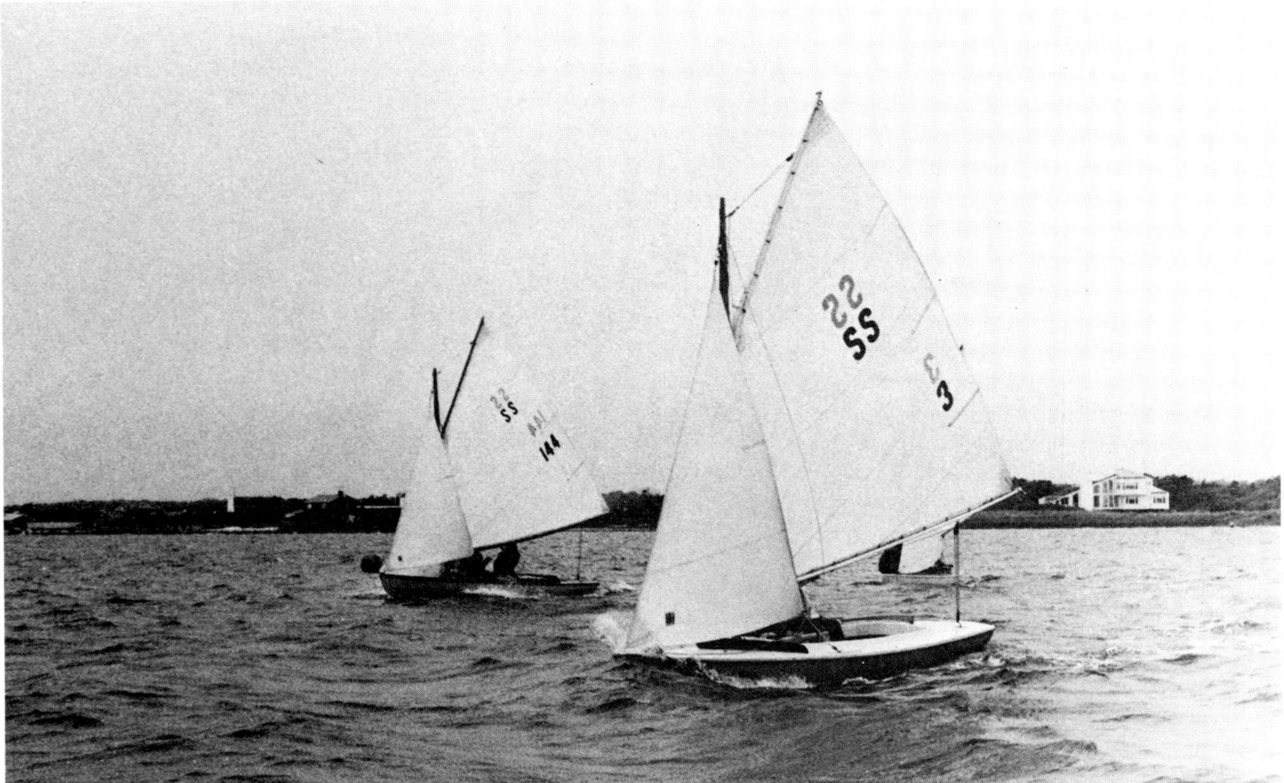
SS
3
SS
144

Today the SS races at Westhampton and Moriches Bay Yacht Clubs. There are three interclub events sponsored by the SS Association at Quantuck, Westhampton, and Shinnecock Yacht Clubs. Racing is a family tradition with son and grandson, daughter and granddaughter fighting to uphold its honor. Many champion sailors such as Sis Rice and Peter Fenner, Adams and Mallory Cup contenders, have received their early training in an SS.

The class history is long and colorful, full of many interesting anecdotes: of the SS that sailed 250 miles around Long Island, of a boat struck by lightning and others swept miles inland during the 1938 hurricane, of the boat that was used as a front lawn flower planter or the one that was taken to the dump but returned to race again. Then there is the tale of the commodore who, when competing for the coveted Queen of the Bay trophy in the 1930s, dyed each sail a different brilliant color and dressed his crew in white. Over he went in a stiff breeze, discovering to his dismay that the dye wasn't colorfast and the bay and their whites were colorful instead of the sails.

This pretty, finely crafted little sloop has provided a great deal of fun, excitement, and good racing for her many loving owners and crews. It is to be hoped that she will continue to play an important part in racing on Long Island's South Shore for many years to come.

Courtesy SS Class Association

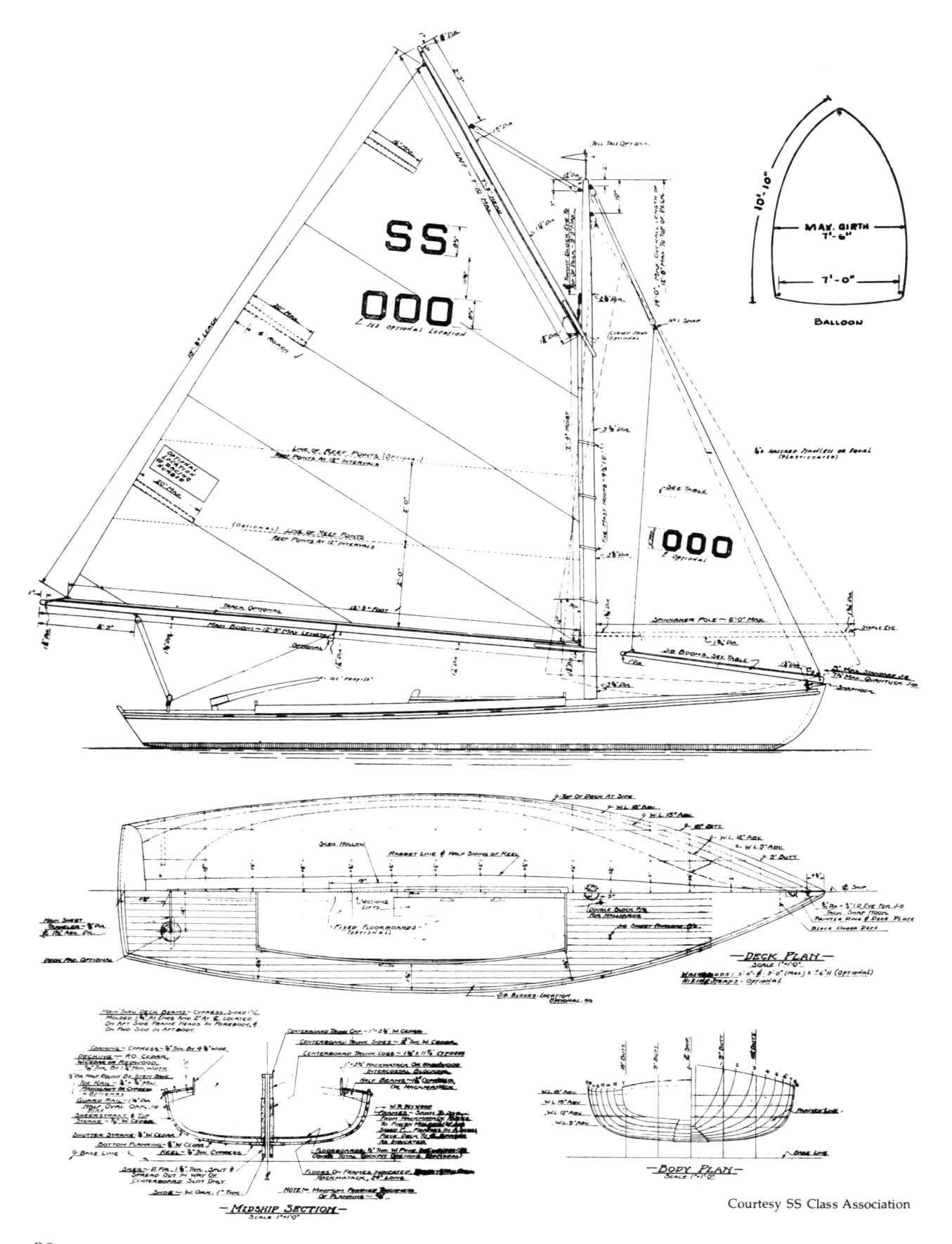

80

The Cotuit Skiff

In Cotuit, Massachusetts, on Cape Cod, a beautiful 14', flat-bottomed, cat-rigged, sailing skiff, known as the Cotuit Skiff, has been racing for seventy-five years. The boat is eye-catching, memorable, with its huge gaff-rigged mainsail and its neat, crisp lined, hard chined, lapstrake hull. Sixty-five or seventy have been built and thirty-five or forty are still active today. Enthusiastic racing of the skiff has always been competitive and exciting, yet the popularity of the class has never spread elsewhere.

The first skiffs were built and raced informally in the early years of the century, before a yacht club with the intriguing name of the Cotuit Mosquito Yacht Club was founded in 1906. Stanley Butler, a Cotuit native, apparently built the first three boats at the request of Dr. Walter Woodman. These were *Trilliam*, owned by the Woodmans, *Robert Kay*, owned by the Channing family, and *Frolic*, which belonged to Rolie Nickerson. The next boats to come along were Bill Taussig's *Swastika*, the Putnams *Topsy II*, and *Kayoshk*.

The building and racing of skiffs probably suggested the formation of the yacht club, and the first owners of skiffs were prominent in it, with Alice Channing first commodore, Anna Woodman, treasurer, and James Putnam, secretary. The remarkable history of the Cotuit Skiff is intertwined with that of a unique yacht club. Not only was the club's first commodore a woman, but it is and always has been strictly a young people's organization. Even today, its voting members must be under twenty-five years of age and unmarried.

The formation of the club spurred on the building of skiffs. At least a dozen had been built by the start of World War I. Most of these were built by Butler, but a few were built by Daniel Crosby. They were not strictly one-designs because Butler enjoyed experimenting. For example, on the first three boats the upper strake was wider than the lower one. On the next three boats this was reversed so that the lower strake was wider than the upper.

Active racing took place before the war. The first cup was presented by Judge Frank Lowell for an obstacle race around nearby Grand Island. In 1911 the Challenge Cup was presented by Dr. Woodman. In 1913 it became the permanent Woodman Challenge Cup after it had been won three times and redonated by Bill Taussig. Races usually started off Woodman's pier with the mast of Dr. Woodman's sloop as one end of the starting line.

After the war, Stanley Butler moved to Nantucket to go into the fishing business. He continued to build skiffs for Cotuit, turning out a group of boats in 1923. In 1924 he built another batch of five skiffs for which he

Courtesy Anna M. Murray

Above: The Cotuit Mosquito Fleet at Woodman's Pier, 1909. Right: Skiffs at Cotuit, early 1900s.

Courtesy Anna M. Murray

made the centerboards out of metal. These boats with "tin centerboards," as they were called, were faster than those with wood boards, and the Yacht Club was forced to introduce a handicapping system. The slowest boats which were built by Crosby started first, followed by Butler's boats with wood centerboards, then Butler's "tin centerboards."

In 1925 Butler built two more metal-centerboard boats of lighter construction which were even faster than his first. Two other deviant boats were also designed and built privately. It was apparent that standardization was necessary. Butler declined the task of drawing up and building boats from standard plans. His fulfillment had always been in his innovations. Naval architect J. Murray Watt was retained and he took measurements off *Scamp,* one of the latest wood centerboarders, and drew up the plans for what has been the Cotuit Skiff one-design ever since. The first boats using these plans were built by Reuben Bigelow of Monument Beach in 1926. He and his son, Cecil, built skiffs until 1950. Other builders in the late 1940s and 1950s were Henry Chatfield Churbuck, Leonard Peck, and Victor Boden.

Cotuit Skiffs racing today.

Dorothy I. Crossley

The Cotuit Skiff measures 14'4¾" overall and 13' on the waterline according to the 1925 specifications. Her beam is 5'1⅞" and she draws 5" with centerboard up. She has a 17'3" boom and carries 144 sq. ft. of sail area in her single mainsail. The 1925 specifications call for white oak frames (such as they are in a boat of this type), white cedar cross planking, canvas over pine decking, oak stem, stern, rudder, tiller, centerboard, and cockpit coaming, pine or fir keelson and deck beams, mast of Douglas Fir and boom and gaff of seasoned spruce. When the plans were revised in 1954

Pin Oak, built and raced by Leonard Peck, was the last skiff to be constructed (1959).

Courtesy Anna M. Murray

Dressed up skiffs during the Eisenhower campaign, August, 1952.

85

by naval architect Edwin H. Mairs, the dimensions were changed somewhat and substitute woods were permitted for the sake of economy.

The Cotuit Skiff is certainly not an easy boat to sail, but it surely is exciting. The huge gaff-rigged mainsail with a boom that overhangs the stern by nearly 4' means that she moves well in light air. It also means that she will be devilish in a blow. Her hull is so shaped, with its flat bottom and hard bilges, that there is a point of no return when she's heeled over. In heavy wind she becomes very difficult to control. She yaws before the wind and sometimes gooseneck jibes. It is sometimes necessary to lower the peak in order to keep on a downwind course, but if one can manage her she surely will move out.

Today, fifteen or twenty Cotuit Skiffs normally turn out for those races which are open to all. The schedule is a busy one, with junior races for those under sixteen on Wednesday afternoons, senior races for those between seventeen and twenty-one Friday afternoons, and open Saturday and Sunday races. Saturday morning races include the Grand Island Race, the Narrows Race, and the Long Distance Race, as well as five Championship Series Races. Saturday afternoon races include three Challenge Cup Races, and special, colorfully named races, such as the Treasure Hunt and the Pirate Game, mostly for children. The Informal Series, originally the Old Man's Series, is held on Sunday afternoons. In addition, there are special races on the Fourth of July and on Labor Day (the Club Championships), the Governor's Bowl Race, and a Blue Water Series to and from the Hyannis Regatta. (During the 1920s and 1930s the fleet sailed to the

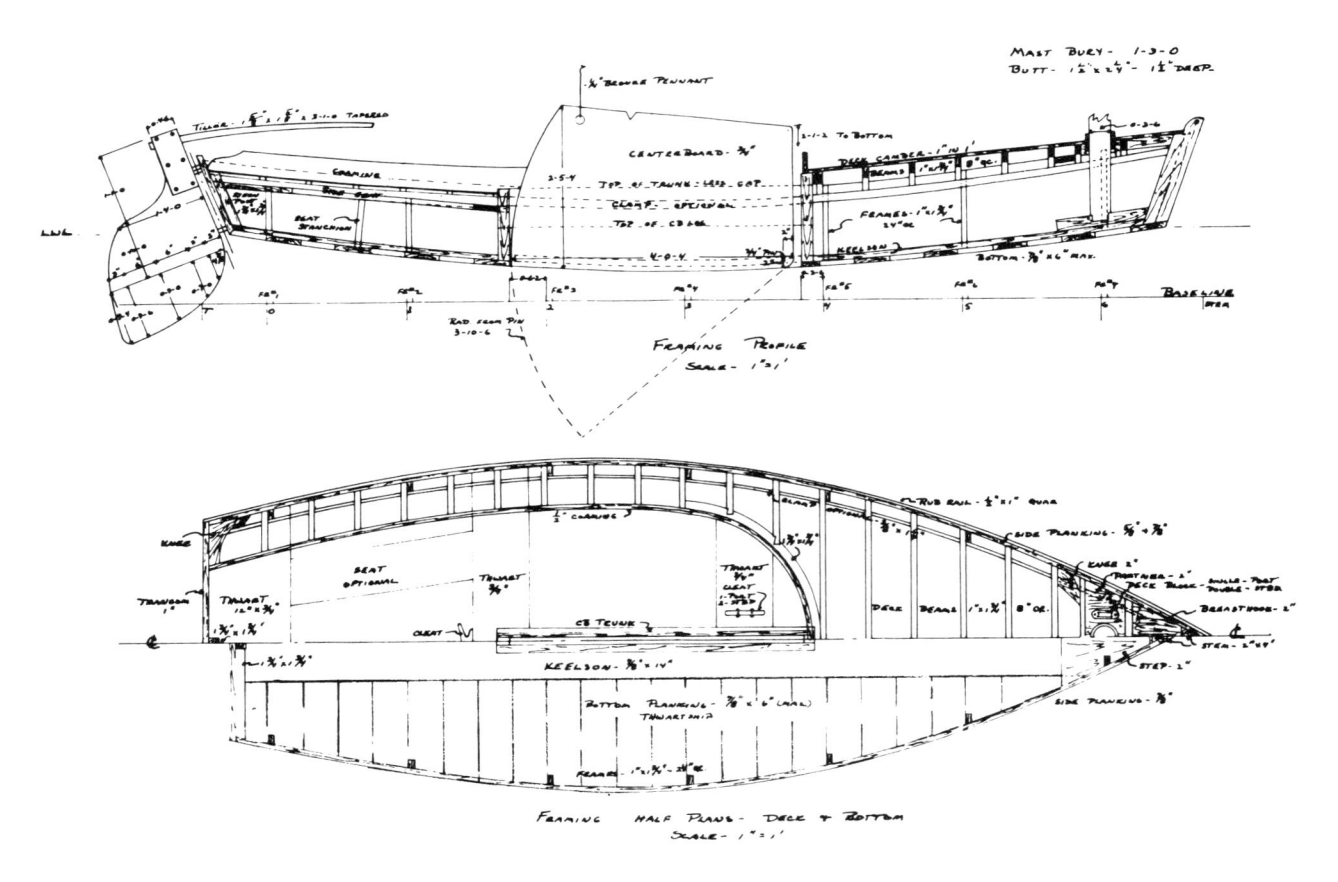

Edgartown Regatta on Martha's Vineyard, a considerable distance over unprotected waters.)

Vixen, built by Cecil Bigelow in 1948, has been donated to Mystic Seaport by Dr. Benjamin V. White. She is a fine example of Cape Cod's oldest racing class, a class which continues to provide fun, challenge, and excitement for her skippers and crews.

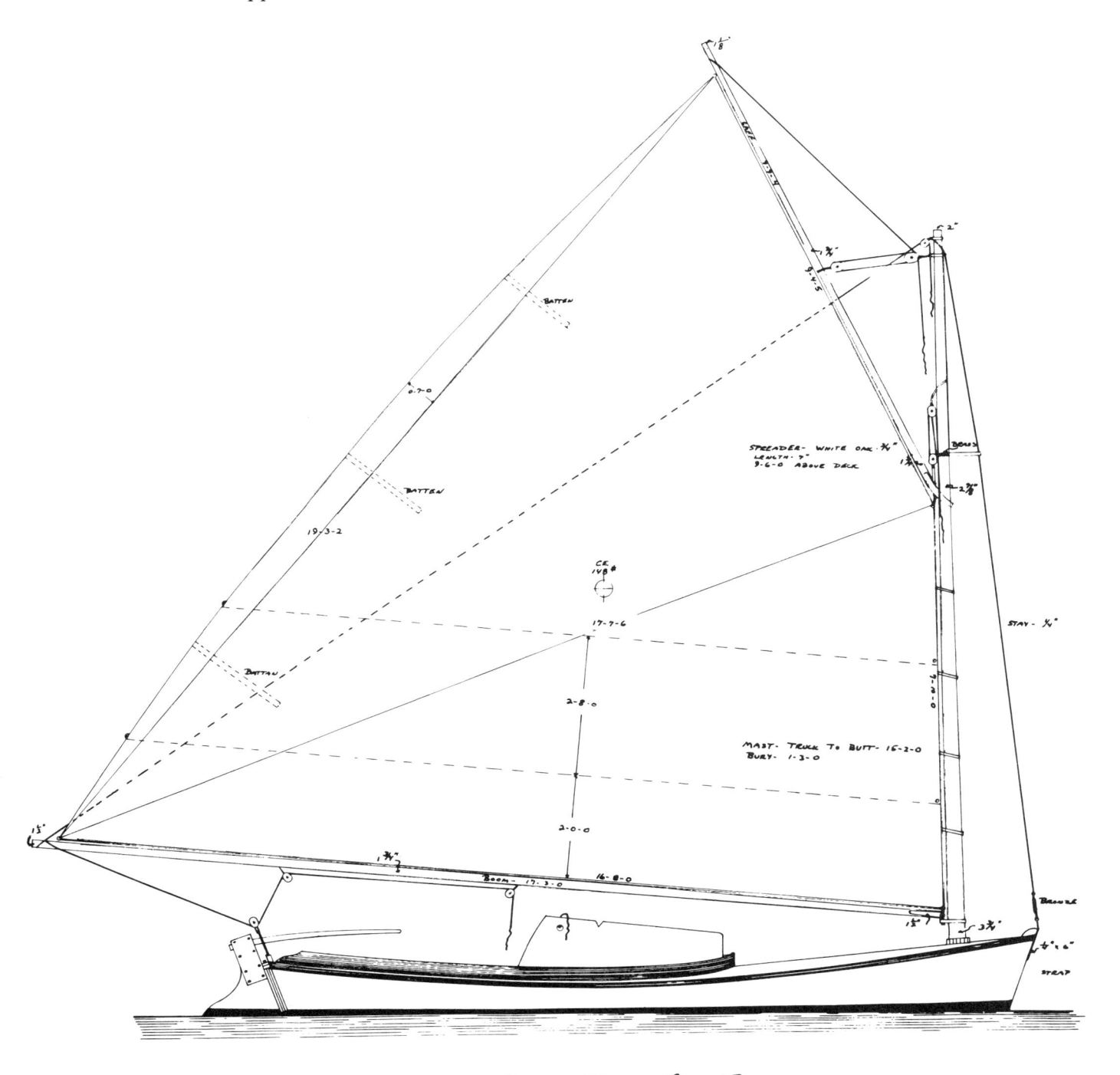

Cotuit Skiff plans redesigned by Edwin H. Mairs from originals by J. Murray Watts

The Luedtke Catboat

On Lake Huron, at Alpena, and Thunder Bay, Michigan, a class of catboats that originated at the turn of the century, or before, is still racing. These boats, known today as the Luedtke Cats, have had a long and interesting history.

The Luedtke Cat began its life on Lake Erie, Lake St. Clair, and the Detroit River. Charles D. Mower was responsible for the design of many of the early boats, which were not strictly one-designs. The hull design which he created was carried through to later versions. These boats had been around for some years when, in 1908, President Taft presented a cup to the Toledo Yacht Club, Toledo, Ohio, as a catboat prize and from then on for some time they were called Taft Cup Catboats in his honor. In the mid-1920s Rudy and Rick Luedtke of Toledo, the builders of the boats, began to make changes to Mower's design. The brothers changed the rig to attain greater efficiency, and the boats became known as Luedtke Cats. They were also known as CK-class and K-class Catboats, CK indicating that the boats were owned by the club where they were raced, and K that they were privately owned.

The class became extremely popular. The Detroit Yacht Club fleet grew from 24 in 1928 to 62 in the early 1930s. There were 150 or more sailing in four classes on Lake St. Clair and the Detroit River about this time. The design probably became standardized in the late 1920s. In 1936–37 N. Zimmer drew up plans. The class was called simply the Inland Lakes Yachting Association or the DYRA (Detroit Yacht Racing Association) One-design Class Catboat.

Between 1954 and 1956 Alpena and Thunder Bay, Michigan, sailors bought twenty-six of the Luedtke Catboats from the Detroit Yacht Club, the Detroit Boat Club, the Edison Yacht Club (Detroit) and private owners on the Detroit River and at Toledo. And so, as is only proper for a cat, the Luedtke continued with its lives.

The Luedtke Catboat measures 22' overall and 17'6" on the waterline, with a beam of 8' and draft of 2'3". The keel and framing are of solid oak. The planking is California Redwood or cedar or mahogany if the owner chose. The coaming, centerboard box, and transom are mahogany. The tiller is hardwood, often walnut. The early boats had wooden centerboards, but later versions have a keel with a steel centerboard which drops down through. A small cuddy cabin was added in the 1920s.

Originally the boats were gaff-rigged, but in the early to mid twenties most changed over to a Marconi rig. The Luedtke brothers were instrumental in this. They increased the height of the mast over a period of years to 36' so that the boats carried a notorious 270 sq. ft. of sail. The boom was shortened and the rig came inboard. The boats carry this rig

Courtesy George E. Van

today. Needless to say it is fast. The Cats will do extremely well in light air and will reach a speed of from seven to ten knots in a fair breeze. They are noted for windward ability, and were particularly favored because of this in the Detroit River where they were adept in the strong currents. The compromise keel with centerboard arrangement helps to maintain stability. It was found, however, that additional ballast was necessary with the earlier centerboard design.

The hull's rounded bilges, ample freeboard, and beam makes it quite comfortable in most sea conditions. The large deck forward, which is about one-third the overall length of the boat, catches the spray. F. G. Luderer,

Courtesy George E. Van

Detroit Yacht Club owned Catboats race on the Detroit River.

Courtesy R. C. Zeidler

Luedtke Catboat in front of the Detroit Yacht Club in the early 1950s.

in Schoettle's *Sailing Craft* reports "In a recent race, 1926, in a strong wind of 33–35 miles, in the Richardson Cup races at the Toledo Yacht Club, Toledo, Ohio, they went through the heavy seas in able fashion. The skippers jibed around the course marks successfully. Outside of shipping

Photo by Clem Mason

Cats return in Thunder Bay River, Alpena, Michigan, after a race on Thunder Bay, Lake Huron.

some water (unavoidable), no damage was encountered by any of these craft in this severe test."*

At a time when she might well be retired the Luedtke Catboat has brought more than twenty-five additional years of racing and sailing pleasure to the sailors of Alpena and Thunder Bay. Several hundred persons have learned the art of sailing her. Today ten continue to race on Wednesdays and Sundays and at the Inland Lake Yachting Association Regatta at Put-in-Bay on Lake Erie. Here's hoping there's yet another life for this beautiful cat.

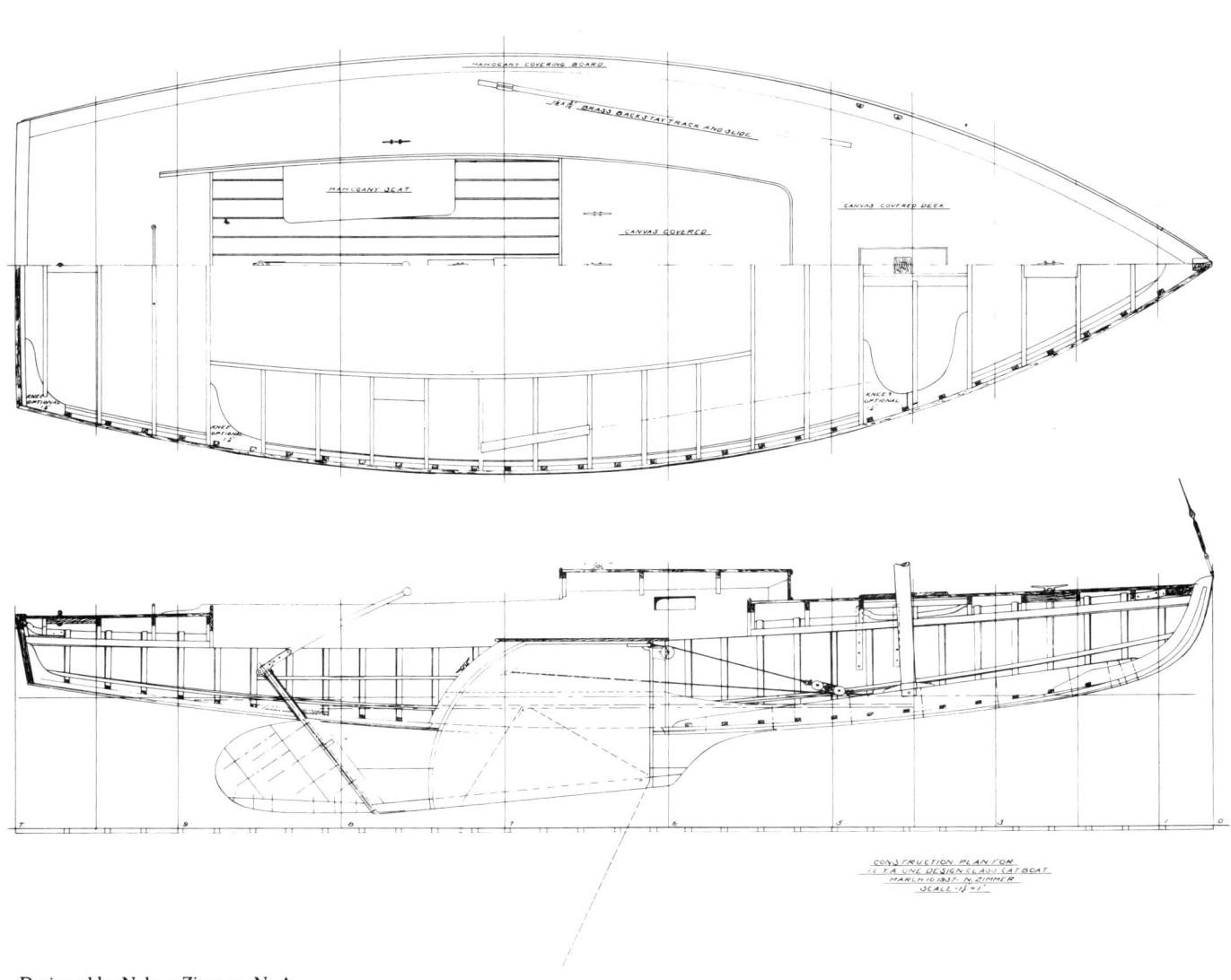

---

*F.G. Luderer, "Taft Cup Catboats," in *Sailing Craft* ed. Edwin J. Schoettle (New York: The Macmillan Co., 1928) p. 450

Designed by Nelson Zimmer, N. A.

Designed by Nelson Zimmer, N.A.

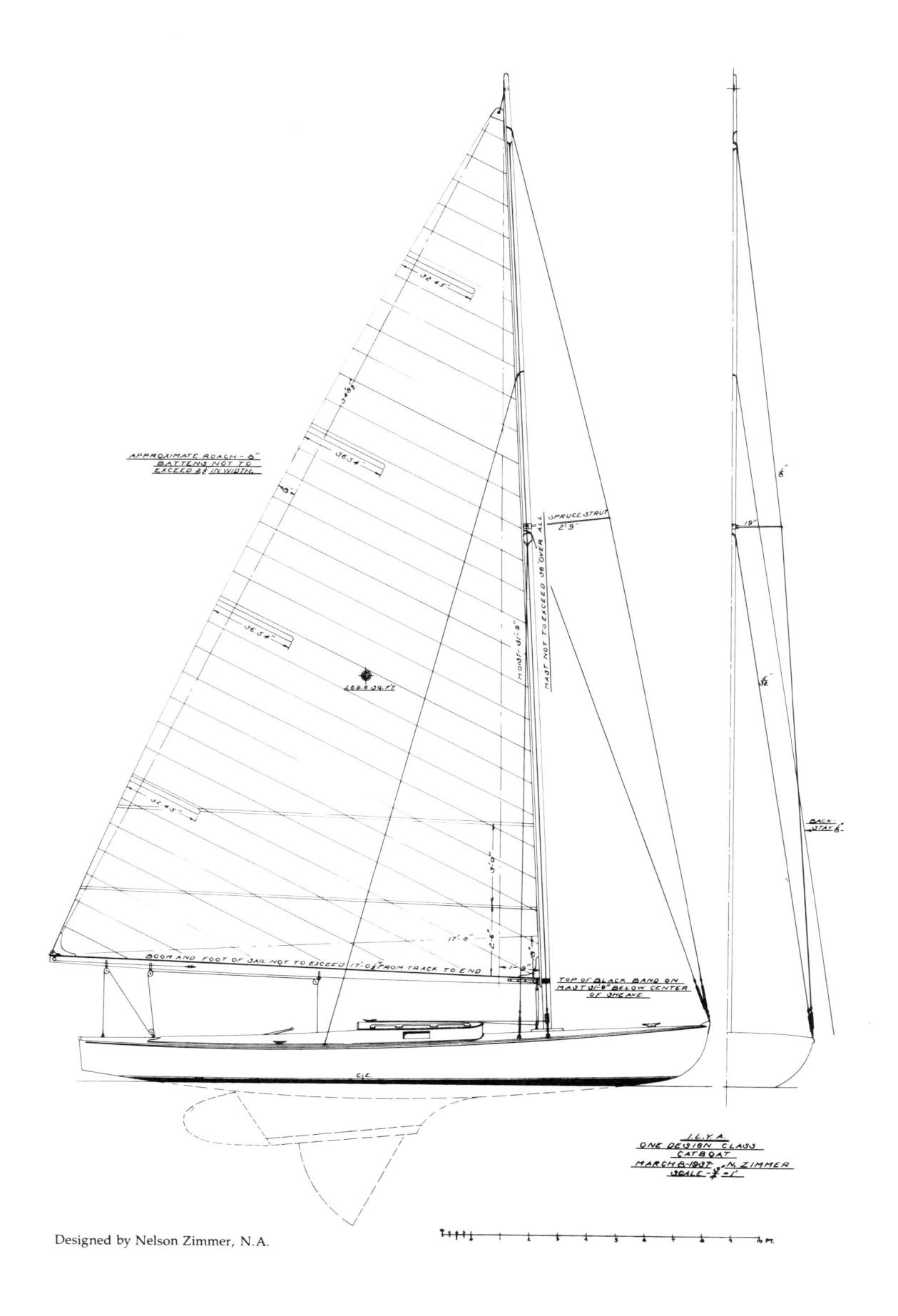

The Herreshoff S

Nathaniel Herreshoff's Standard S Class Sailboat is a standard of excellence in every way. She was "built to last a lifetime," according to the Herreshoff Manufacturing Company catalog, and it is true. Sixty to 70 of the original 101 or 102 boats built are still sailing, with nearly 50 still racing. The quality of construction is still very much in evidence, and so are her fine sailing qualities. She is noted for speed in light air, and for the ability to "take it" when the going gets rough, a rare combination of traits. The S is thought to be the first one-design class to carry the Marconi rig.

The first Herreshoff S was built by the Herreshoff Manufacturing Company, Bristol, Rhode Island, in 1919 for Paul Hammond of Oyster Bay, on Long Island, New York. The boat was not intended as a one-design, but nine more like it were soon built, and the class became popular. Thirty-four boats were built by 1925, and fleets were established at the Seawanhaka Corinthian Yacht Club, at Oyster Bay, at the Pequot Yacht Club in Connecticut, at the Eastern Yacht Club, Marblehead, Massachusetts, and at the Bar Harbor Yacht Club, Bar Harbor, Maine. An additional 51 boats were built between 1925 and 1930, bringing the total at that date to 85. Other fleets were formed in Massachusetts at the Corinthian Yacht Club, Marblehead, at Quisset and Newport, Buzzards Bay and at Vineyard Haven, Martha's Vineyard, and in Rhode Island at Newport. Five boats built in 1928 were shipped to Honolulu, Hawaii, and the navy built an additional two there shortly before World War II. The last S was built in 1941. Of the 101 or 102 built, 95 of these were constructed by the Herreshoff Manufacturing Company and 5 or 6 were built by George Lawley and Son, Neponset, Massachusetts.

The fleet at Oyster Bay became dispersed over western Long Island Sound, and the Long Island Sound Fleet was formed in 1939 when racing began off Larchmont, New York. A fleet was also formed in Narragansett Bay, Rhode Island, after the war. Both of these, as well as a small, less formally organized fleet at Sorrento, Maine, are active today. The largest fleet is that at Narragansett Bay, which is made up of twenty-six boats, with nine at the Edgewood Yacht Club, four at Tiverton, two at Newport, and others elsewhere. The fleet races sixteen Narragansett Bay Yachting Association races as well as five pre- and five postseason races. The Long Island fleet numbers eighteen boats, with five sailing out of the Larchmont Yacht Club, six at Horseshoe Harbor Yacht Club, others at Sea Cliff Yacht Club, Hempstead Harbor, and elsewhere. Ten boats or more are at the start for the thirty-two races of the Yacht Racing Association of Long Island Sound Mid-sound Series. Lively competition has existed between the Narragansett Bay and the Long Island Sound fleets since the late 1940s. A

Danaé Associates

National Championship Series and Team Racing are hosted annually by one fleet or the other. The fleet at Sorrento, Maine consists of five or six boats which were bought up from the Bar Harbor fleet when interest began to wane there in the late 1930s. Other boats which are not engaged in active racing may be found in Massachusetts, California, Mystic, Connecticut, in the Chesapeake Bay area, and in Hawaii.

The specifications for the S are: length overall 27'6", length on the waterline 20'6", beam 7'2", draft 4'9", sail area approximately 425 sq. ft., displacement 6,750 lbs. Ballast is approximately 3,350 lbs. of lead on the

Danaé Associates

keel. The S is framed in oak and planked in ¾" cedar, secured with bronze screws. The keel is also oak. Trim is varnished mahogany, oak, or teak. Spars are of clear spruce, the mast being hollow and other spars solid. Sails include a mainsail, a jib and a spinnaker. An S is easily recognizable by her curved mast, the bow of which is most pronounced in the upper half.

The Herreshoff S is beautifully balanced; she can be steered with one finger. She is responsive and will move in the lightest of breezes. Her speed is something to be reckoned with. It is not uncommon for her to do five knots in a ten-knot breeze, and to do better than her theoretical hull speed of a little over seven knots. She is initially tender, but once laid over she has tremendous stability. An avid Long Island Sound S sailor says "It takes eighteen–twenty knots to put the rail on the water with the mainsheet traveler at its racing center position; and by letting the traveler to the rail (a capability not provided in the boats as built) and easing the headstay to let the mast sag aft, you can drive the boat in twenty-five knots, and should survive thirty–thirty-five without damage if the sea isn't too bad. No reef points on any sail I've seen down here in the last ten years."

S boat sailors also point out the boat's versatility. Not only is she a first rate one-design racing boat, she is an excellent "camping cruiser," and her large, comfortable cockpit provides for ideal day sailing.

From the Narragansett Bay Herreshoff S Class Association Yearbook published in 1969 on the fiftieth anniversary of the S Class: "It is abundantly clear to those who have had the privilege of owning and racing S Boats that her designer, Nat Herreshoff, knew his business and knew it well. From the fair lines of her hull to the responsiveness of her helm she is a thoroughbred. To sail an S Boat on a dusty day and to feel her drive and stability or to glide effortlessly by much larger yachts when there is seemingly little wind at all, is to know and comprehend the full range of the S Boat's excellence."

E.L. Goodwin/Cape Cod Shipbuilding Co.

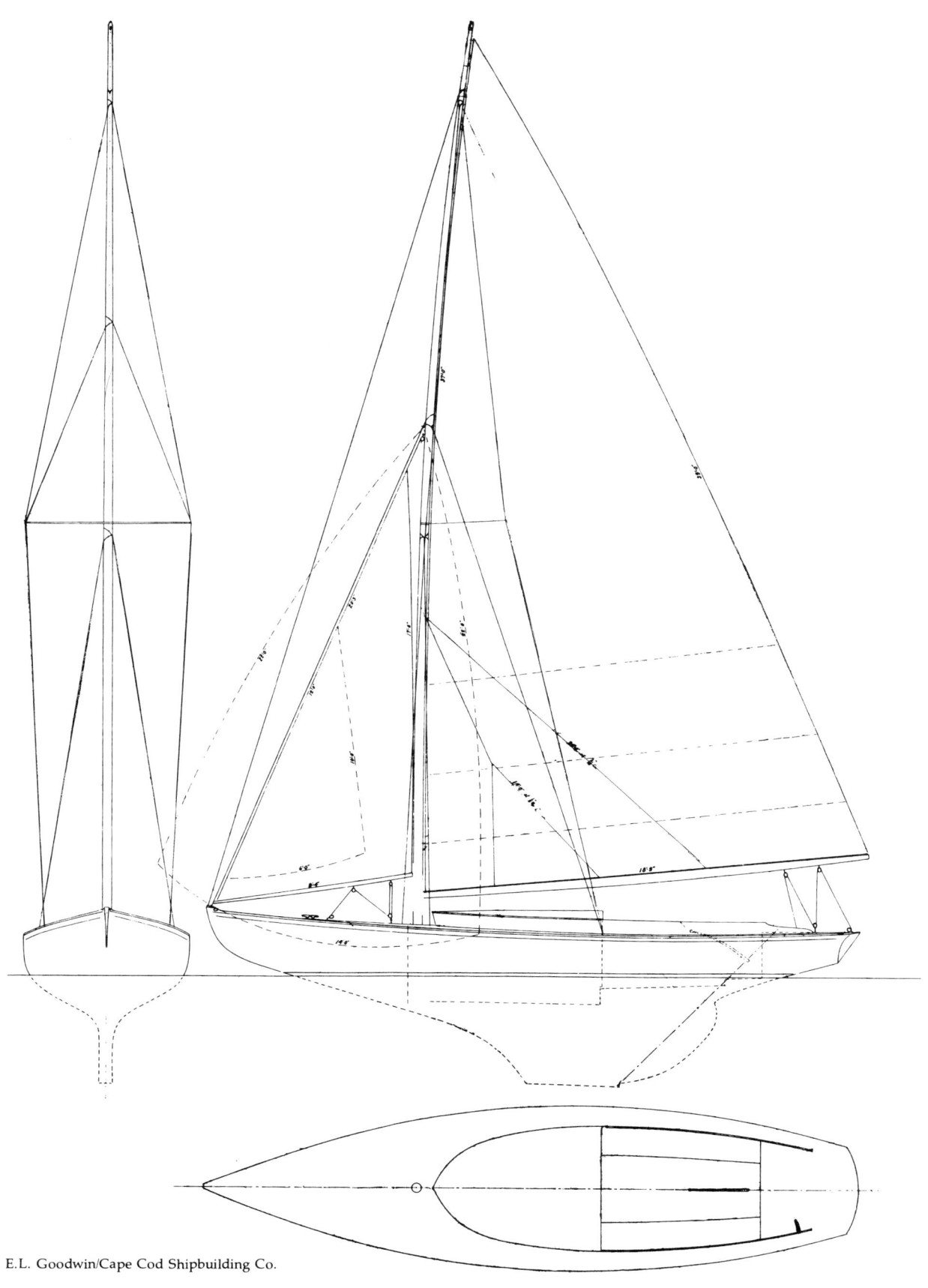

The Massachusetts Bay Hustler

The Hustler has been one of Massachusetts Bay's most popular and well-known classes. It seems as if practically anyone who has owned a boat in the Boston or South Shore, Massachusetts area has owned a Hustler, at one time or another, and can tell all about them. This fine performing, 18' catboat has changed the mind of many a catboat skeptic.

Charles D. Mower designed and built the first Hustlers in the winter of 1924. In the spring of 1925 he took three of them from Swampscott to Winthrop to show to some of his friends. Among them was a veteran sailor by the name of George Floyd, who became instrumental in starting the Hustler class. Floyd tried out one of Mower's boats, liked it, and bought it. He convinced his friends and they purchased five other boats for the Winthrop Yacht Club. This was the beginning of the Winthrop Hustler class.

These six boats drew considerable attention in the interclub series. However, the jib and mainsail rig was gaining popularity at the time and most people weren't interested in a catboat. For ten years Floyd in his boat, *Huskie* and the others in their Hustlers struggled along, trying to draw attention to the boats by painting them bright colors and giving them names that all began with *H*. In 1936, another popular veteran like Floyd, Fred Sterling, of the Squantum Yacht Club, decided to get out of the overcrowded Indian class and bought a Hustler. That was the turning point. Suddenly everyone wanted a Hustler. In the next six years, before World War II broke out, the class increased from six boats to the point where thirty-five to forty boats were at the line for the interclub events. Fleets were formed at other Massachusetts Bay clubs, such as Wollaston, South Boston, Quincy, and Wessagussett Yacht Clubs. After the war, the Hustler class continued to grow in numbers until it reached a peak in 1954 when eighty-eight boats were racing in three interclub fleets. The class has declined since then, but with the acceptance of fiberglass for hull construction in the 1950s, the number of Hustlers is beginning to increase again.

Today the only active fleet is at the Wollaston Yacht Club, but individual Hustlers come out from the other Massachusetts Bay clubs to compete in the interclub races. One hundred seventy-seven boats have been built, thirty-one of which are fiberglass. Although few of the wood boats still race, perhaps forty are still afloat. Some eleven or twelve wood Hustlers have been gathered together at Town River, Quincy, Massachusetts, where they are lovingly cared for and are informally raced.

With the exception of a fleet of fourteen boats built by Mt. Desert Yacht Yard in 1948 and raced for some years at Somesville, Maine, on Mt.

Diane Welsh

Desert Island, the Hustlers have never spread as a racing class beyond the shores of Massachusetts Bay. Individual boats are to be found, however, in such diverse locations as San Francisco and North Carolina.

The Massachusetts Bay Hustler measures 18' overall and has a beam of 6'5½" and draft of 4' with centerboard down, 8" with board up. The sail area is 180 sq. ft. The minimum hull weight is 750 lbs. The wood boats had no frames. They were transversely planked with longitudinal stringers for structural strength. The stringers, ribs, stem, keel, and deck beams, etc., were of oak. Planking was of fir, spruce or cedar.

Hustlers racing in the fog.

Some minor changes have been made to the hard-chine hull design over the years as the plans were revised. The rig was considerably improved in the mid to late 1930s when the mast was cut down from 26' to 21'9" at the hoist. The boat's performance to windward was bettered, and she became faster overall. The cockpit has usually been rectangular, but was rounded and extended all the way to the transom in some of the early boats.

The introduction of fiberglass hulls and aluminum masts has contributed greatly to the preservation of the Hustler as an active racing class. The fiberglass boats have not improved performance dramatically; the better-maintained wood boats are still competitive. The 1978 Massachusetts Bay Hustler Association National Championship, in which twenty-two Hustlers competed, was won by a twenty-five-year-old wood boat.

The most attractive feature of the Hustler is its sailing performance. The boat is a simple design that is easily balanced and extremely stable even in winds exceeding twenty-five knots. Its upwind ability is unmatched for a boat of its size and weight.

The Hustlers have been mainly "backyard built" by people who knew boats and could read a blueprint. Even today the fiberglass boats are built in lots of four or five and everyone pitches in to finish them off. Racing and building has often been a family matter. Those who have brought up families racing in the Hustler praise it highly as an excellent family boat and say that it has provided a great way to "bring up the kids."

Wood Hustler, *Whyte Cap,* at Town River, Quincy, Massachusetts.

Bruce L. Whyte

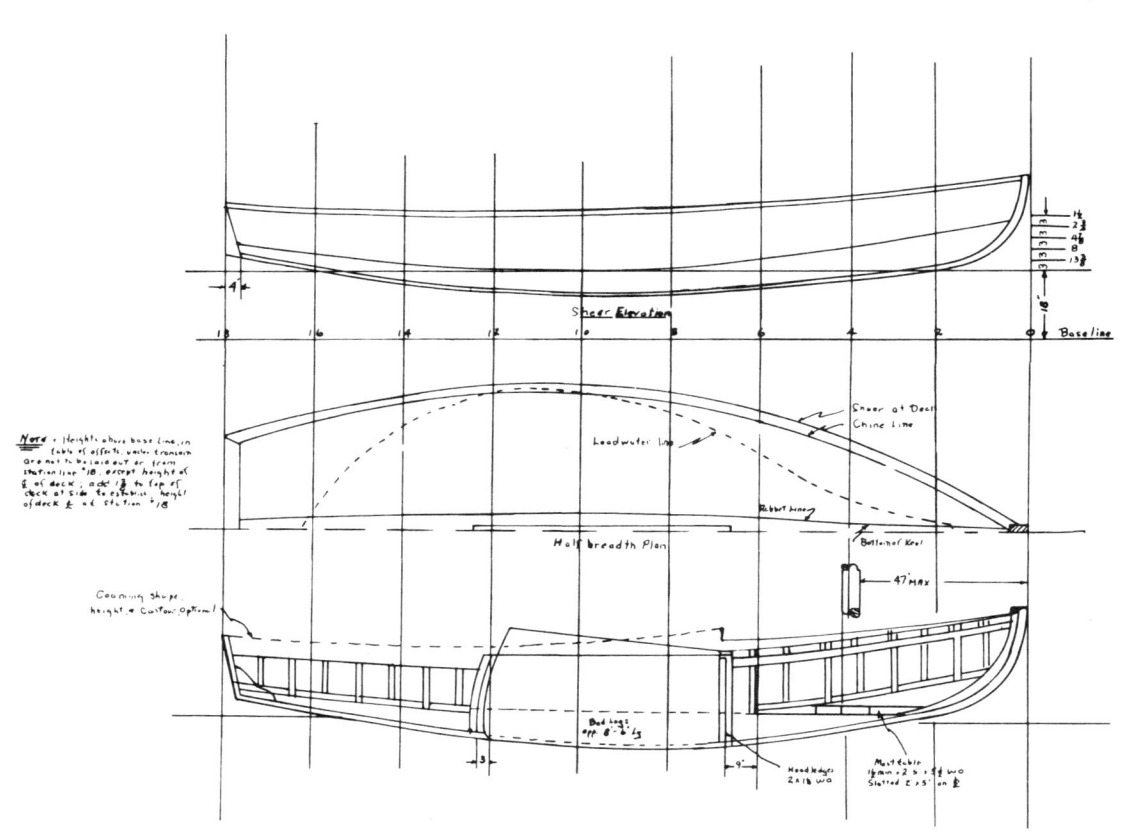

104

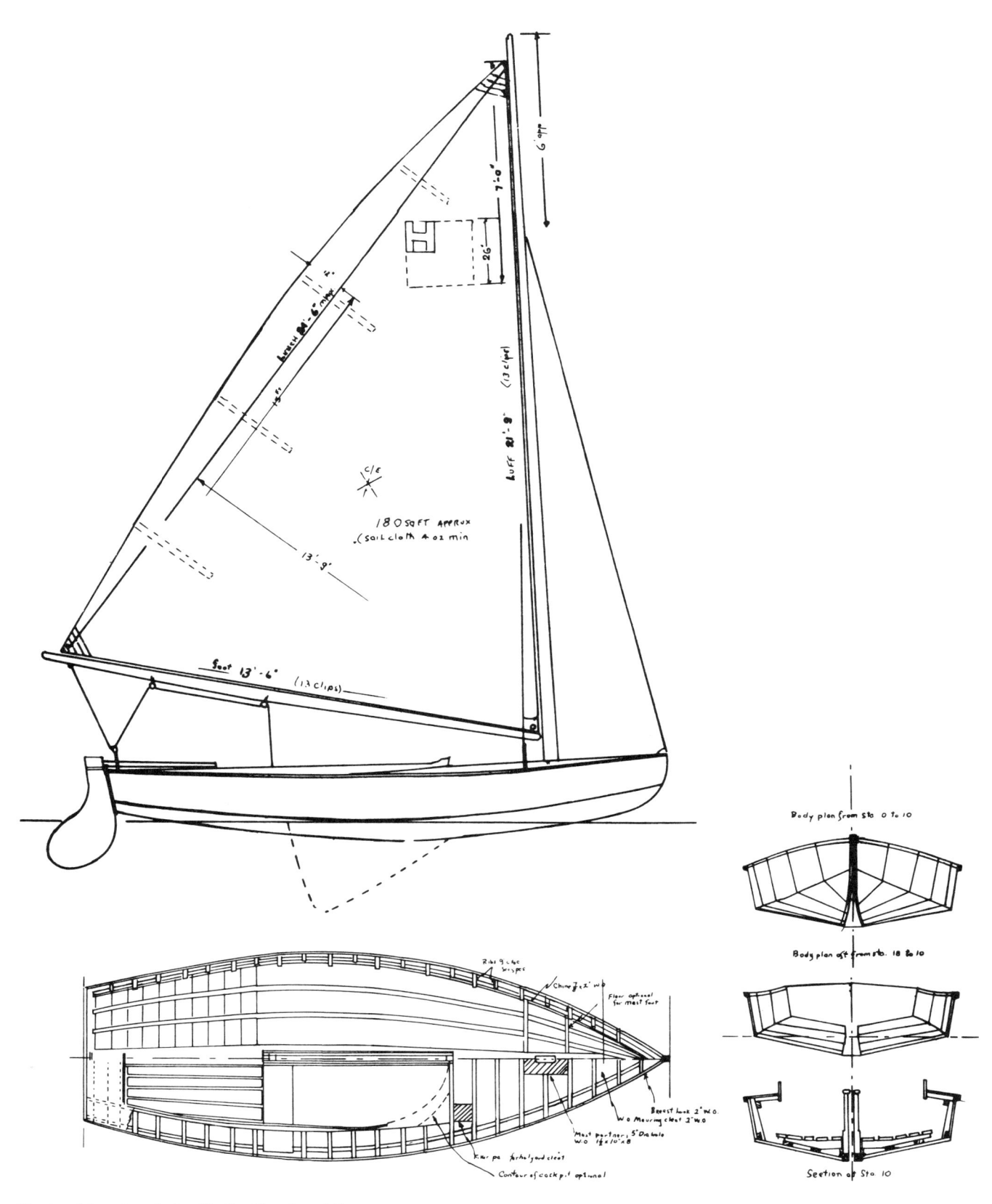

Courtesy Massachusetts Bay Hustler Class Association

105

The Inland Lake Scows

The Inland Lake Scows are spectacular racing machines, renowned for their phenomenal speed. The earliest date back before the turn of the century, long, long before planing hulls and multi-hulls became popular. Today, instead of diminishing, the Scows are increasing in numbers, with fleets appearing all over the United States and Canada. A great deal of credit for the Scows' incomparable history goes to the Inland Lake Yachting Association, which in 1978 celebrated its eightieth birthday. It is this organization which has nurtured the development of the Scows, and has promoted and controlled Scow racing.

The history of the Inland Lake Scow and that of the Inland Lake Yachting Association go hand in hand. The ILYA was founded January 28, 1898 in Milwaukee, Wisconsin to represent clubs in Illinois, Indiana, Minnesota, and Wisconsin. At just about the same time the first Scow was designed and built. Up until the time when the Association was founded, racing on the inland lakes had been chaotic. Boats of varying sizes were raced in two general classes, one for catboats and the other for sloops, under an almost impossible handicapping system. It was obvious that uniformity of classes was necessary. There was also a desire for interclub racing and an annual regatta, for common rules and organization. It was the ILYA that brought about all this.

The first annual regatta was held beginning August 22, 1898, at White Bear Lake, Minnesota. Two classes were established, one not to exceed 20', the other not over 17'. The winners of the five-day regatta were *Mahto*, sailed by Lucius Ordway, Sr., in the 20' class, and *Xenia*, sailed by H.T. Drake, in the 17' class. Both boats were built by White Bear boat builder, Gus Amundson.

In 1895 or thereabouts, Ordway had discussed the theory of a flat-bottomed boat with Nathaniel Herreshoff, and in 1896 Herreshoff built the *Alfreda* for Milton Griggs of Minneapolis, with Ordway making the arrangements. This boat was almost a Scow, as was the *Mahto*. But neither was built as the true Scow came to be; with ribs across the bottom and no keel. It was John O. Johnson, another White Bear boat builder who had worked for Gus Amundson before going into business for himself, who built the first real Scow. *Dominion*, a double-hull boat from Montreal, which was built like a canoe, had attracted attention when it successfully defended the Seawanhaka Cup, and Charles A. Reed, a member of a New York architectural firm, had worked on a design for a single-hull version. Johnson built his boat from this plan, but put in twin bilgeboards instead of a centerboard. Apparently the owner of this first Scow wasn't farsighted enough to appreciate it, for he named the boat *Weirdling*. He took out the twin bilgeboards and returned to a centerboard.

Courtesy ILYA

Class E Scow

Whatever the merit of the first Scow, the idea caught on. The tremendous possibilities for speed with this design were recognized. By 1900, classes A and B had come into existence. The A Boat, as it was called, could not exceed 38' in length, or carry more than 500 sq. ft. of sail. Bs were smaller, their length not exceeding 32' and carrying less than 350 sq. ft. of sail. By 1903 the Scows were reasonably well established, the ILYA had a home at Oshkosh, Wisconsin, and was working to control the Scow classes as one-designs. Popularity grew fast. The C Scow came along in

Maynard Meyer Collection

Class A Scow Regatta at Pewaukee Lake circa 1908.

1906. It was a 20' catboat. In 1924 the 28' E Scow replaced the B Scow, which had died out. The M, M–20, MC, and others have come along much more recently.

The Inland Lake Scows have a long, narrow, almost rectangular hull which has practically no draft. They move over the water, not through it, and are intended for shallow or sheltered areas where the seas can't build up. Twin bilgeboards on each side of the cockpit run through the hull to provide stability. The Scows make their best speed when heeled consid-

Courtesy ILYA

Class A Scow with modern Marconi rig.

109

Courtesy ILYA

Class C Scows

erably, and twin rudders are used to maintain control. The early Scows were originally gaff-rigged, but today all Scows are Marconi-rigged. All but the A, which is no longer built, are constructed of fiberglass. Principal builders are Melges Boat Works, Zenda, Wisconsin, and Johnson Boat Works, White Bear Lake, Minnesota.

The Scows sail at incredible speeds of twenty to twenty-five knots and more. As might be expected, they are tremendously exciting to sail and race. Some of them can be physically exhausting, the A being the most taxing. Before hiking straps, it was necessary for skipper and crew of a C Scow to ride the windward bilgeboard in a good breeze.

Today there are still about ten A Scows competing. The Cs and Es number over 1,000. A few years ago the Scows were raced only on the lakes of the Midwest and in Barnegat Bay, New Jersey. Today they may be found from coast to coast. The ILYA represents fifty clubs in Wisconsin, Minnesota, Illinois, Iowa, Missouri, Indiana, South Carolina, Texas, Michigan, and Kansas. It is likely that the Scows will continue to grow in popularity. The epitome of excitement and sport they provide insures that few Scow sailors will be interested in sailing any other boat.

Courtesy ILYA

Class E Scows

STANDARD HARDWARE PLACEMENT

MELGES CLASS C SCOW — in Fiberglass

SCALE: ¾"=1'-0"

E Scow

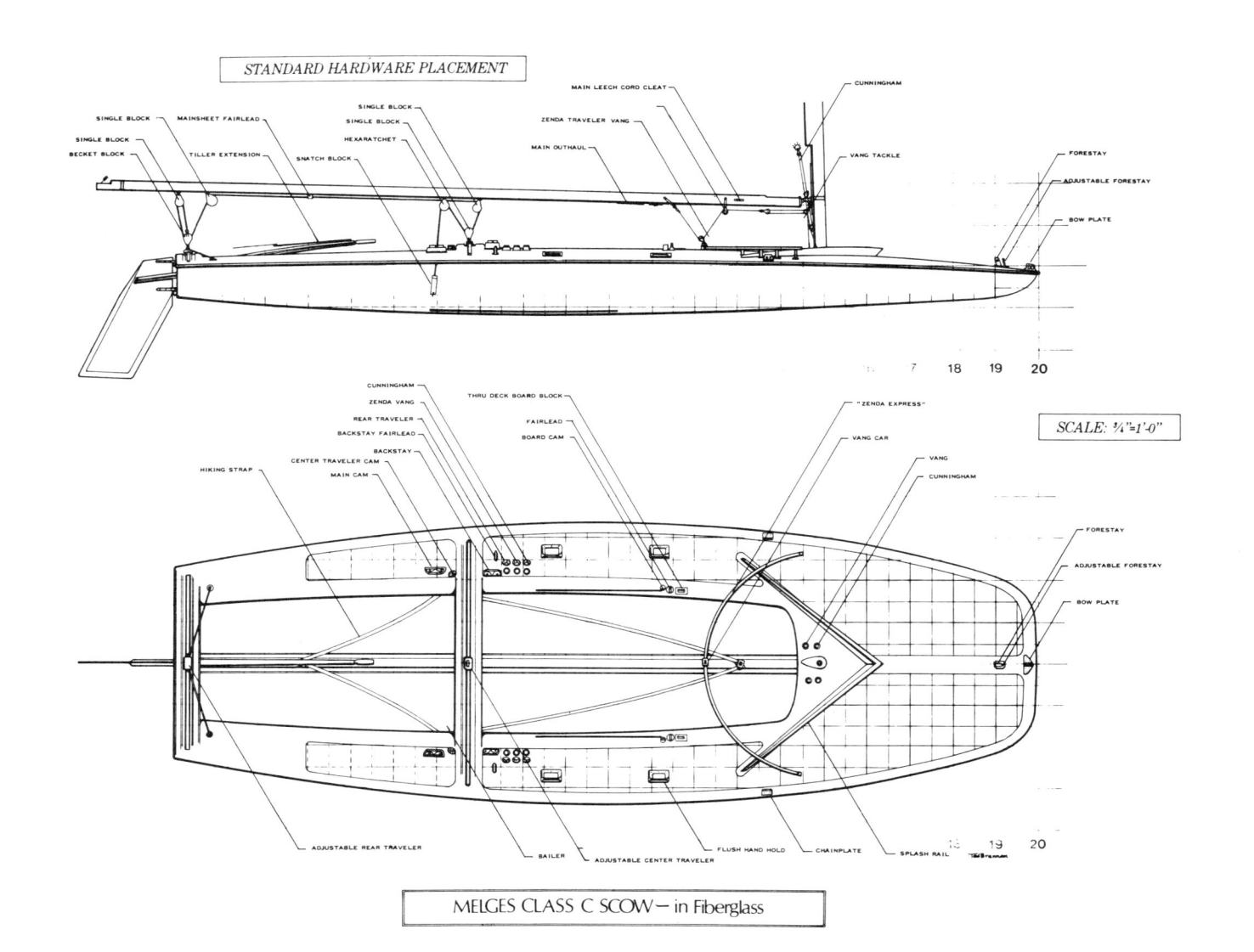

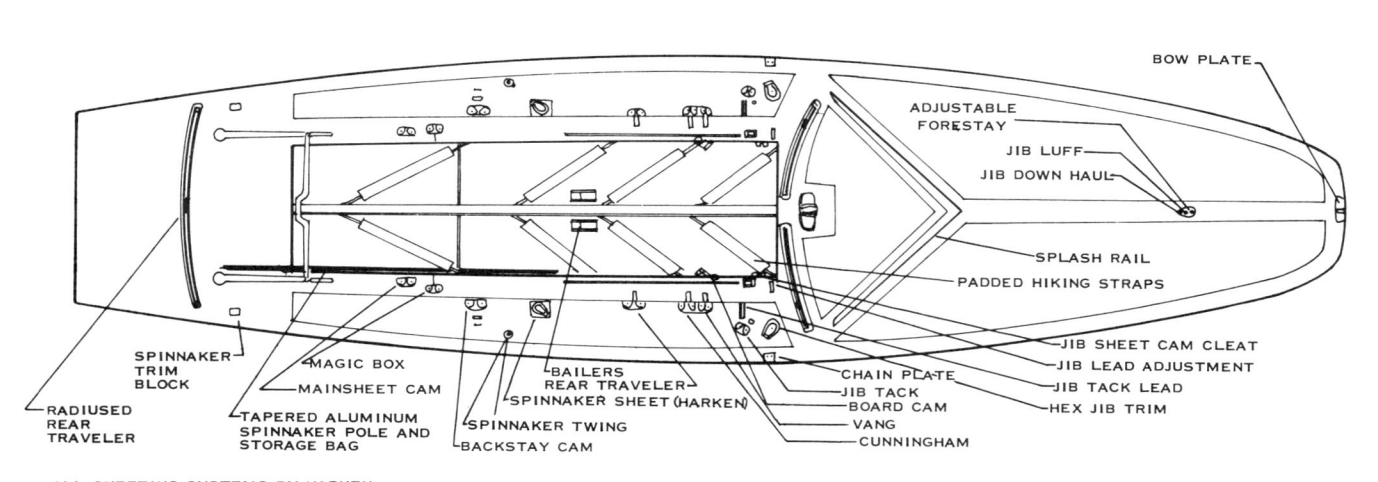

ALL SHEETING SYSTEMS BY HARKEN
CUNNINGHAM, VANG, REAR TRAVELER
EASILY ADJUSTABLE FROM HIKING POSITION
COLOR-CODED BRAIDED LINES THROUGHOUT

Courtesy Melges Boat Works

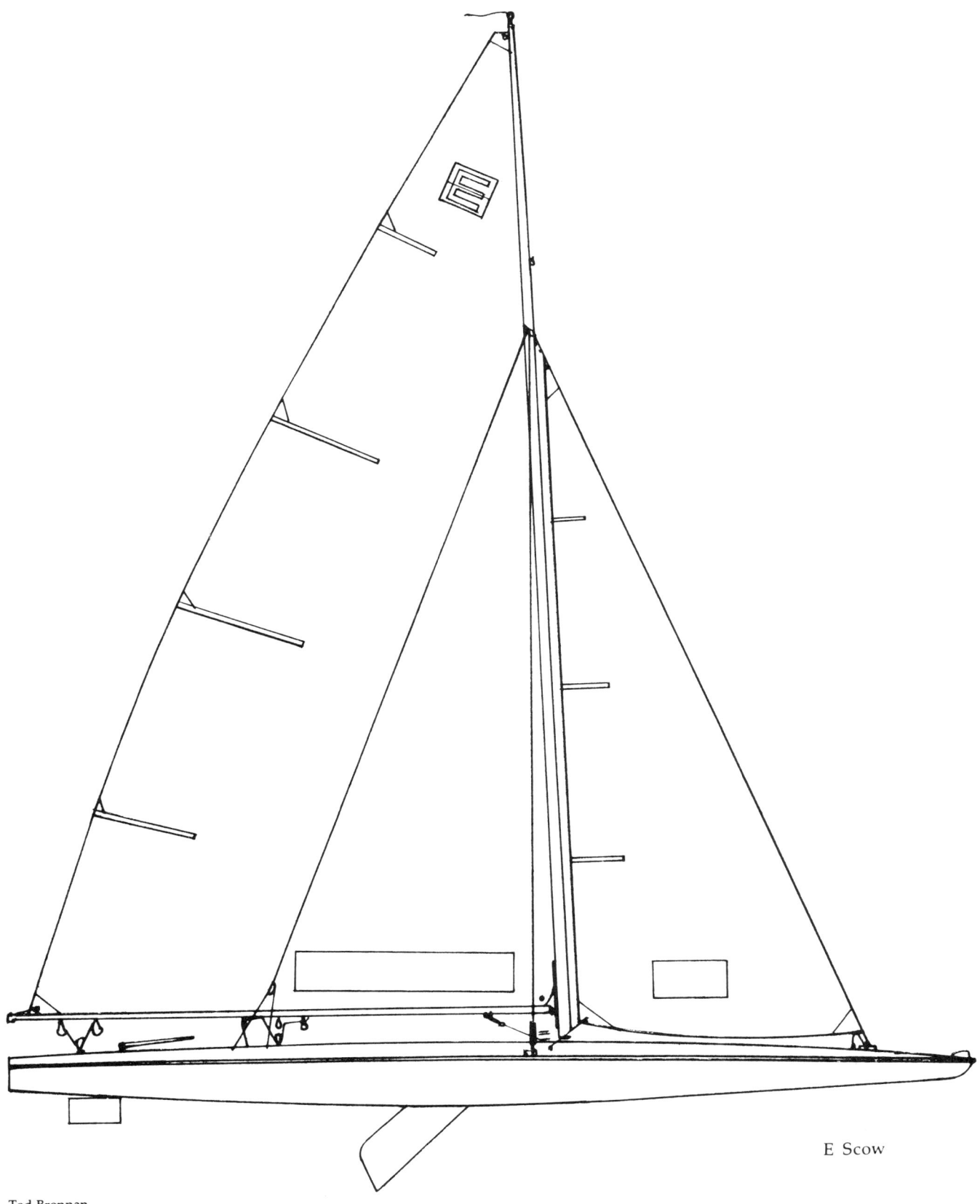

Ted Brennan

E Scow

The Herreshoff 15
(Buzzards Bay 15, Watch Hill 15)

At Watch Hill, Rhode Island, a Marconi-rigged version of one of the very earliest one-designs, Nathaniel Herreshoff's well-known and well-loved 15 Footer, is not only still racing, but has been given a new lease on life with the addition of fiberglass hulls to the fleet. Although the rig of the Watch Hill 15, as it is called, is very different from that of the original gaff-rigged Herreshoff 15 designed in 1898, the hull varies only in minor dimensions. The exquisite beauty, the excellent sailing characteristics, and fine construction have produced a kind of charisma, "an admiration almost akin to idolatry in the minds of those who owned, sailed, and raced these boats."*

The first 15s were designed for members of the Beverly Yacht Club, Marion, Massachusetts. The club had become disenchanted with the never-ending problems of handicap racing and desired a class of like boats. The committee of members who commissioned the design was headed by noted yachtsman R. W. Emmons II, who was well known to Nathaniel Herreshoff. Eleven boats were built during the winter of 1898–99. They were personally delivered the following spring by Herreshoff, who towed them to Marion behind his steam yacht, *Squib*. Lots were drawn for their distribution to their new owners. In the ensuing years the class became very popular. Perhaps seventy were eventually built. They appeared and raced elsewhere in Buzzards Bay and Rhode Island, but nearly all were originally built for the Beverly Yacht Club, and their concentration there was almost a monopoly. At Beverly they were the E class and were commonly called Es. They were also known as the Buzzards Bay 15. Today, only a few are still in existence.

One of the early Es, *Fiddler*, built in 1902, has been donated to Mystic Seaport by her owner, Augustin H. Parker. Interestingly, *Fiddler* was originally owned by Mr. Parker's mother, Caroline M. Dabney, who must have been one of the first yachtswomen. In 1904 Miss Dabney and *Fiddler* won the Beverly Yacht Club championship. In 1933, Mr. Parker and *Fiddler* won the Van Rensselaer Cup, given to the winner of an open handicap race which could be entered by any sailing yacht in Buzzards Bay, and *Fiddler* was not the first or the last 15 to win this prestigious trophy.

In 1922 members of the Watch Hill Yacht Club requested a Marconi-rigged Herreshoff 15. The Watch Hill 15s were built by Herreshoff during the winter of 1922–23. As with the original 15s built twenty-four years before, there were eleven of them and they were towed to their destina-

---

*David Cheever, "The Herreshoff Fifteens," *The Log of Mystic Seaport*, Summer 1972.

tion, the Watch Hill Yacht Club, where they were tied up at the dock. Distribution was by matching numbers sent to each new owner with those on a card on each boat. No additional 15s were built. The eleven were actively raced until the 1938 hurricane destroyed four of them. One boat was rebuilt by using the port side of one wreck and the starboard side and keel of another. The seven survivors continued to race.

In 1968, a group of Watch Hill sailors who had owned and loved the old boats formed a syndicate to rebuild the fleet. Unsuccessful attempts were made, in both the United States and in Europe, to locate a reasonably priced builder to construct the hulls out of wood. Fiberglass was the affordable alternative. The yacht *A Movable Feast* was used as the plug for the mold, which was made by Alan Vaitses Boatyard, Mattapoisett, Mas-

Courtesy David Cheever

Herreshoff 15s racing during the first season, 1899, before they had been numbered.

sachusetts. Again, there were eleven boats in the new fleet, built in 1969–70. These joined the three remaining originals and they continue to race, old and new together, today.

The original Herreshoff 15 measured 24'6" overall and 15' on the waterline, with a beam of 6'9" and draft of 2'6" with centerboard up and 5'6" with board down. Displacement was approximately 2,800 lbs. The keel-centerboard arrangement was a "compromise sloop" design. The centerboard was raised and lowered through a slot in the keel, which had a moderate draft. This permitted the boat to manage with board up in the shoal areas which are prevalent in Buzzards Bay, but to have the advantages of a deep keel where conditions allowed. Lead ballast on the keel was about 1,000 lbs.

Herreshoff changed the hull design only slightly for Watch Hill. Principal differences are in the freeboard, which is a bit greater, and the transom, which is somewhat deeper. LOA, LWL, beam, etc., were nearly identical.

Start of a 1904 race. E-11 is *Fiddler*, now at Mystic Seaport, raced by Caroline M. Dabney, and an all girl crew, which won the Beverly Yacht Club Championship that season.

Courtesy of Mystic Seaport Museum, Mystic, Conn.

116

The Herreshoff 15 was framed in white oak, and planked in 9/16" Washington cedar fastened with brass screws. The hull was very lightly, yet strongly, constructed. Stem, keel, plank floors, deck beams, centerboard, rudder, and coaming were of oak. Deck planking was of Washington cedar and the transom was butternut. Traditional finishing was white topsides, green bottom, cream or tan decks, white interior, and varnished seats, coaming, toerails, cockpit sole and tiller. The original hulls had two watertight bulkheads, one forward and one aft, to provide positive flotation. In many instances these were opened up for storage purposes, which was probably good for the health of the hull because it permitted air circulation.

Watch Hill 15s racing in the 1930s. Note Alden O boat in right background.

Photograph by Hubbard Phelps

Photograph by Hubbard Phelps

Fiberglass Watch Hill 15 with new, modern rig.

Sail area for the gaff-rigged Herreshoff 15 was about 330 sq. ft., comprised of about 257 sq. ft. of mainsail and 73 sq. ft. of jib. A spinnaker or balloon jib of about 147 sq. ft. was also carried. Apparently Herreshoff experimented with the rig on the early boats, as sail areas vary considerably. The original sails were made by the Herreshoff Manufacturing Company from Egyptian cotton. The jib was clubfooted and could be self-tending, though it was rarely rigged this way.

The original sails for the Marconi-rigged Watch Hill 15 were made by Ratsey. The jib was also club footed and the spinnaker was triangular. When the new fleet of fiberglass boats was built, a completely modern rig of 296 sq. ft. was designed by Sandy Van Zandt of Vanzant Sails, Old Mystic, Connecticut. The spar is 3' taller than the original and the boom is 2½' shorter. The jib is loose footed and overlapping. There is a radial

Kelly Pickering

Original, gaff-rigged Herreshoff 15, *Mistress*, owned by Raymond Coleman, summer 1978.

spinnaker. The old boats do amazingly well against the new rig, however, largely because of the excellent downwind ability of the old rig.

The Herreshoff 15s are noted for their fine sailing characteristics: for speed, stability and ability to carry sail, balance, and seaworthiness. The Marconi rig has considerably improved windward ability and speed. The gaff-rigged original, however, was very fast for its time. It is still noted for light air and downwind speed, and versatility. It can be reefed down and still give excellent performance in heavy seas and winds. David Cheever writes in his article, "The Herreshoff Fifteens" (*The Log of Mystic Seaport* Summer, 1972) "We reach the buoy and round it, slack off the boom, settle the peak and now comes decision. The spinnaker boom is full fifteen feet long. The big flat-cut spinnaker is masthead and the running back-stays go just above the jaws of the gaff. We are in the middle of the fleet. We can't win. In short, we are crazy to set a spinnaker at all. The boat next to us makes no move to set hers. One of those ahead has scandalized hers by tying a canvas stop part way down the sail, thus reducing its area by one third. We say a prayer and break ours out full. Leaping ahead of the

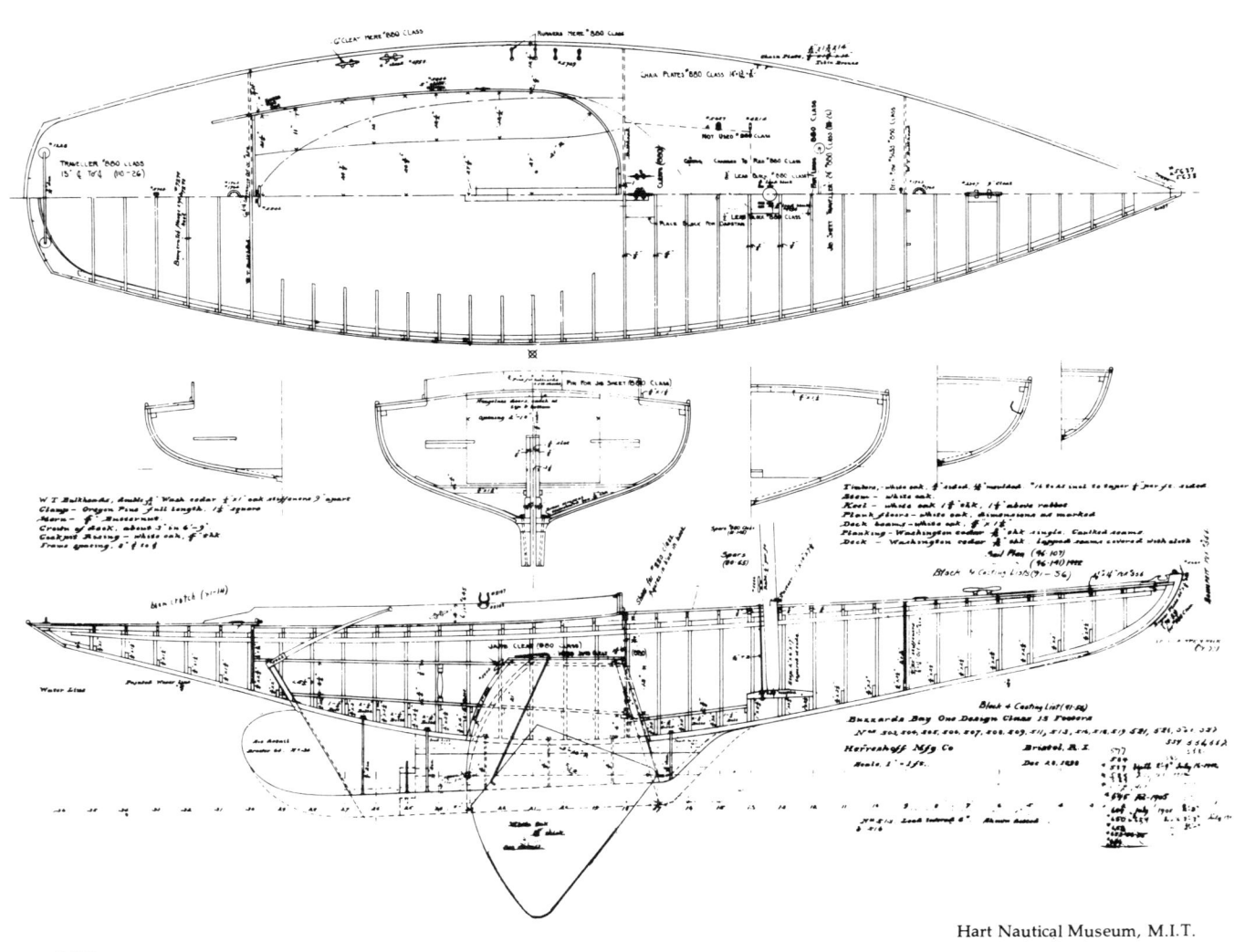

Hart Nautical Museum, M.I.T.

boat next to us, we start after our short-spinnakered friend. The unstayed upper portion of the mast has a curve like a buggywhip. Then she does it. Suddenly and without warning—but just as hoped—she catches a sea under her lovely Herreshoff stern. She starts to surf. This is no scow-type boat. This is a full-bodied hull moving beyond its designed speed. At moments she is throwing her spray from the back stays, which means that fully fifteen feet of her hull is suspended over the seas. She quivers and vibrates while we shout with excitement."

Is it any wonder the love of these fine classic boats approaches idolatry?

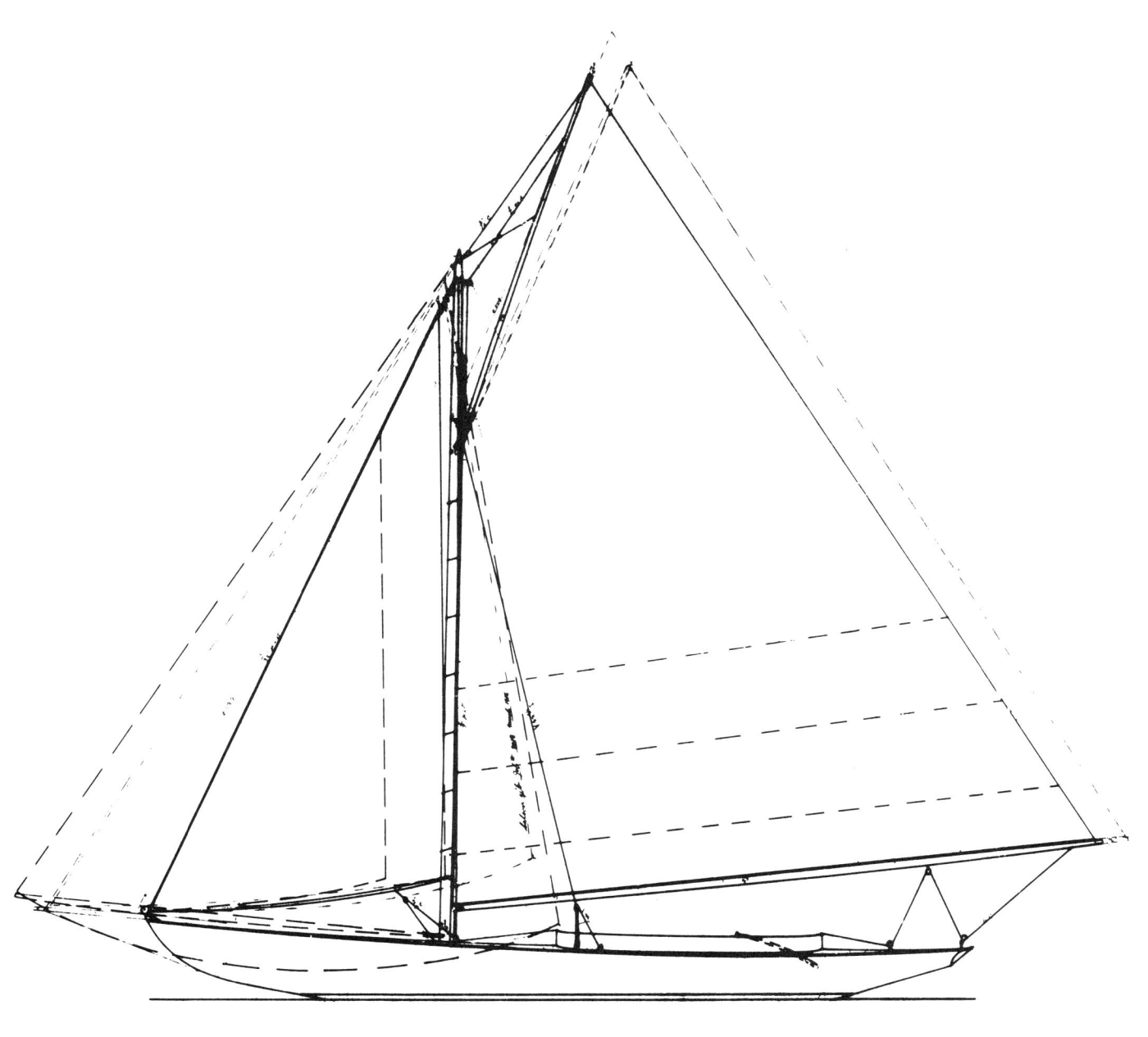

Hart Nautical Museum, M.I.T.

Other Early One-Design Classes

The Duxbury Duck is an 18′ Marconi-rigged sloop designed by John G. Alden in 1925. It is a centerboard boat designed specifically for the shoal waters of Duxbury Bay, Massachusetts. Twenty-four were built by George Chaisson of Swampscott, Massachusetts in 1925, and the class numbered about sixty boats in Duxbury by the late 1930s. There were smaller fleets at Plymouth and Crystal Lake, Wakefield, Massachusetts. The Ducks raced into the 1960s at Duxbury and a number are still in existence.

Specifications: 18′ LOA, 15′1″ LWL, 6′4″ beam, 7″ draft with centerboard up, 2′6″ draft with board down.

The Brutal Beast was designed by E. Starling Burgess in the early 1920s for Marblehead, Massachusetts youngsters. It is a 14′, hard-chined, V bottom, centerboard catboat, which was originally gaff-rigged and later converted to Marconi. It became extremely popular, and many well known yachtsmen got their early training in it. There were four divisions, comprised of twenty-five to thirty boats each, racing in Marblehead by 1937. The class also spread to Blue Hill, Maine, and Orleans, on Cape Cod. It is said to have been named for Burgess's Great Dane, whom his Marblehead neighbors nicknamed "Brutal Beast". There have been some plans for reviving the class in fiberglass.

Specifications: 14′ LOA, 6′2″ beam, sail area 127 sq. ft.

The Indian, a popular Marconi-rigged, centerboard sloop, was designed by John G. Alden in 1924 for the Squantum, Massachusetts Yacht Club. Around 100 were built and a number are still around. The class was well known on Massachusetts and Narragansett Bays, and on the Connecticut shore. It was last raced on Massachusetts Bay in 1970.

Specifications: 21′2″ LOA, 16′9″ LWL, 6′4″ beam, 18″ draft with centerboard up, 3′6″ draft with board down, sail area 230 sq. ft.

The Pumpkinseed is a gaff-rigged sneakbox type design that has been raced at Long Pond in Plymouth, Massachusetts since 1924. The first boat came to Long Pond from the Great Lakes. It was taken overland to Maine and then sailed down the coast. After summer residents had founded the Chetolah Yacht Club they chose this boat as the model for the class of sailboats to be raced. Six were built in the winter of 1923–24. By 1933, twelve had been built, and by 1948, twenty-three. The latest boats (highest hull number is 31) were built in the mid-1960s by George Davis of Plymouth Marine. Today about twenty still race, including several of the first boats.

Specifications: 14'4" LOA, 4'6" beam (approximate—specs vary slightly according to builder).

The Wianno Junior is a smaller sloop design by H. Manley Crosby, who designed the Wianno Senior. It was originally gaff-rigged, but later changed to Marconi. About eighty were built by Crosby Yacht Building and Storage Company, starting in 1921. The boats were raced on Cape Cod by juniors under eighteen years of age until the 1960s. They were last raced at the Wianno and the Hyannisport Yacht Clubs. Many were destroyed by hurricanes, resulting in their replacement with other small fiberglass classes. There are still a number in existence.

Specifications: 16'6" LOA, 13' LWL, 6' beam, 1'6" draft with centerboard up, 3'6" draft with board down, sail area 139 sq. ft.

The Herreshoff Sixteen Footer (Fish Class) is a keel sloop designed by Nathaniel Herreshoff in 1916. It is a larger, roomier version of the Herreshoff 12½. The boats were originally gaff-rigged, but as with the 12½, a Marconi rig was later offered as an option. Nearly forty were built, of which perhaps twenty are still active. The class raced on Long Island Sound, on Narragansett and Buzzards Bays, and at Portland, Maine. A few Fish have recently been built in fiberglass by Justin Camarata of Noank, Connecticut.

Specifications: 20'9" LOA, 16' LWL, 7'1½" beam, 3'1½" draft, sail area 270 sq. ft.

The Victory is a raised deck, Marconi-rigged keel sloop designed in 1920 by William Gardner for the Larchmont Yacht Club, Larchmont, New York. Twenty were built by Henry B. Nevins of City Island, New York. The class name, Victory, was chosen as a tribute to World War I yachtsmen. All the original names were related to the war; *Ace, Spad, Nieuport,* and so on. Some of the boats were sold out of the Larchmont Yacht Club quite early, to be raced on the Great Lakes. In the late 1940s the Victory was still among the outstanding classes on Long Island Sound, and interclass team races were conducted between it and the Herreshoff S. Perhaps the Victory's most famous sailor was Norman Rockwell. A few, including number 1, *Ace,* and number 18, *Gopher,* are still in existence.

Specifications: 31'6" LOA, 20'10" LWL, 7' beam, 4'10" draft.

The Triangle is a 28' Marconi-rigged keel sloop designed by John G. Alden in 1925. James Graves built eight in 1926 for a Marblehead, Massachusetts fleet, and an additional five in 1927 for a fleet in Jamestown, Rhode Island. A 1928 fire destroyed the original mold, and a new one was constructed. A total of about sixty were built by about 1933 for fleets at Marblehead, Gloucester, Rockport, Eastern Point, and Annisquam, in Massachusetts, at Jamestown, Rhode Island, and near Portland, Maine. Over the years some Triangles were lost in fires and in hurricanes. There are at least thirteen still in existence, including five in Gloucester, Massachusetts.

Specifications: 28'6" LOA, 18'6" LWL, 7'6" beam, 4'9" draft.

The Winter Harbor 21

is a gaff-rigged keel sloop designed and built by Burgess and Packard of Marblehead for the Winter Harbor (Maine) Yacht Club. In the summer of 1906, A.A. Packard surveyed the local sailing conditions, and it is believed that E. Starling Burgess drew up the plans the following spring. Seven boats were built for the 1907 season. An additional two were built in 1922 and 1924 by George Lawley and Son, of Neponset, Massachusetts, bringing the total built to nine. The boats were raced actively until World War II. Interest declined after that. By the 1960s only an occasional race took place. Many of the boats have been sold out of state. Seventieth Anniversary Races were held in August, 1977.

Specifications: 30'8" LOA, 21'3" LWL, 7' beam, 5'2" draft.

The Dark Harbor 12½

is a smaller keel sloop designed by B. B. Crowninshield, designer of the larger Dark Harbor 17½. It was built by Rice Brothers of East Boothbay, Maine, for the Tarratine Yacht Club at Dark Harbor, Islesboro, Maine, in 1915 and 1916. It was originally known as the Islesboro Class. The boats were acquired in the 1930s by the Bucks Harbor Yacht Club. They are still raced there today, as is the Dark Harbor 17½. Eleven are registered with the club.

Specifications: 20'2" LOA, 12'6" LWL, sail area 210 sq. ft.

The Wee Scot

is a 15' Marconi-rigged keel sloop designed by Thomas D. Scott around 1922 and built by Milton Boat Yards, Rye, New York. Around 375 were built, primarily for junior racing. The class was very popular on Long Island Sound where it raced until the mid 1940s. A fleet of 29 boats raced at Sorrento, Maine, beginning in 1926. A smaller fleet of 8 boats also raced at Deer Isle, Maine. The fleet at Sorrento has been revived in recent years. Fiftieth Anniversary Races were held in 1976.

Specifications: 15'3" LOA, 11'3" LWL, 5'3" beam, 3' draft.

The New York Thirty,

one of the most famous one design classes, was designed by Nathaniel Herreshoff for the New York Yacht Club in 1905. Eighteen boats were built. Although large compared to most other one-designs, they were the smallest boats qualified to join a NYYC cruise. Keenly competitive racing by their prestigious owners lasted for about thirty years. Several are still sailing.

Specifications: 43'6" LOA, 30' LWL, 8'10" beam, 6'3" draft.

The Bar Harbor Thirty

was designed by Nathaniel Herreshoff in 1903 for members of the Bar Harbor Yacht Club, Mt. Desert Island, Maine. Thirteen were built. They were raced until 1917 in Bar Harbor waters, and later regrouped in Marblehead, Massachusetts, where they raced into the 1930s. Near the end of their racing days they were converted from gaff to Marconi rig. Several are still sailing.

Specifications: 49'10" LOA, 30'9" LWL, 10'4" beam, 7'3" draft.

The Great South Shore Bay Bird,

a gaff-rigged, centerboard sloop, was designed by Charles D. Mower in 1923 for racing on Long Island, New York's Great South Bay. Twenty were built by S. W. Newey of Brookhaven, Long Island, during the winter of 1923–24. Twenty more were built during the following two winters (ten each winter). They sailed on Moriches Bay, Shinnecock Bay and Mecox Bay, as well as Great South Bay, all on Long Island's south shore. Races were held at Westhampton Yacht Club, Shinnecock Bay Yacht Club, and Mecox Bay Yacht Club. The boats carried bird's wing insignias on the sails, and were named for bay birds.

Specifications: 21'1" LOA, 14' LWL, 6'4" beam, 1'6" draft.

The Atlantic City Catboat was designed by Bowes and Mower in 1913 for the Atlantic City Yacht Club, primarily as a class for its junior members. Ten boats were built by South Jersey Yacht Building Company for Atlantic City. Later boats were built for other Jersey clubs, including those at Ocean City and Cape May. The class also spread to Barnegat Bay. About forty had been built by 1928.

Specifications: 15' LOA, 6' beam.

The Mt. Desert Island Class (commonly called the MDI Class) was designed in 1924 by Ralph E. Winslow. The class was commissioned by Edsel B. Ford and the list of distinguished owners included John D. Rockefeller and Joseph Pulitzer. Ten or twelve of these high-sided, Marconi-rigged keel sloops were built for the junior members of the Seal and Bar Harbor Yacht Clubs.

Specifications: 22' LOA, 17' LWL, 6'8" beam, 4'5" draft.

GLOSSARY

backstay: a cable of rope or wire which is attached to the deck and supports the mast from aft. Running backstays are backstays that may be tightened or slackened while sailing.

ballast: heavy material, such as lead or stones, placed low in a boat to provide stability. Internal ballast is weight placed within the hull; external ballast outside, for example, as part of the keel.

ballast-displacement ratio: the ratio between the weight of the ballast and the total displacement weight of a boat.

battens: strips of wood or other material positioned in pockets in the leech of a sail to extend it and give it shape.

beam: the width of a boat at its widest part.

bilge: the bottom part of the hull where the sides turn into the bottom. The bottom of the hull.

bilgeboard: a board lowered through the hull at the bilge to provide stability.

brightwork: varnished wood.

bulkhead: a vertical partition that separates compartments in the hull.

centerboard: a board set in a casing amidships which pivots from forward and is lowered through the bottom of the boat to provide stability.

chine: the angular intersection between flat sections of a hull.

coaming: raised board around a deck opening that keeps out water.

cockpit: the open area lower than the deck where the helmsman and crew work.

cuddy: a small cabin on a boat.

daggerboard: a board that is similar to a centerboard, except that it is lowerd straight through the bottom of the boat instead of pivoting from forward.

davit: a form of crane for hoisting a boat onto another boat, as a dinghy onto a larger yacht.

dinghy: a small open boat used for rowing, sailing, and often as a tender for a larger boat.

draft: the vertical distance from a hull's waterline to its lowest point.

fin keel: a type of keel, finlike in appearance, which is not an integral part of the hull shape, and is often added after the hull construction is completed.

forefoot: the point where the stem and keel of a boat meet.

frame: riblike structure of the hull to which the planking is attached.

freeboard: vertical distance between the deck of a vessel and the waterline or water surface.

gaff: a spar used to support the head or upper edge, of a fore and aft sail, hence gaff-rigged.

gooseneck: a fitting that secures the boom to the mast. Usually a universal joint.

gunter rig: a type of rig in which a gaff slides up a short mast and becomes an extension of it. The sail has four sides, but appears triangular.

gunwale: the upper edge of the side of a boat hull.

harpings (harpins): pieces joined to the "set-up plank" and running back across the topside ends of the forward ribs at the bow of a hull of sneakbox-type construction. These pieces form the connection between bottom and deck.

headstay: the forward stay which supports the mast.

hiking: to counterbalance the heeling of a hull by climbing or leaning out to windward.

keel: the backbone of a hull, running lengthwise, to which the frames are attached.

keelson: an auxiliary reinforcing structure, usually fastened to the inside of the keel.

knockabout: fore-and aft-rigged sailing vessel marked by the absence of a bowsprit; usually a sloop rig.

knee: an angular piece of timber used in hull construction, usually to secure structural members such as deck beams.

Marconi rig: a type of rig characterized by a tall mast, relatively short boom, and triangular sail. The name Marconi came from the similarity between a telegraph tower and the complicated early rig with spreaders. Sometimes referred to as jib-headed rig.

planking: the hull covering of boards attached to the frames. Carvel planking is planking with butted seams giving a smooth surface. Lapstrake planking is planking with overlapping seams, also known as clinker-built planking.

rudder: a flat vertical piece at the stern of a vessel which directs its course when turned by a wheel or tiller.

reef: to reduce sail area by rolling up and tying down part of the sail. Reef points are places on a sail where the sail may be tied down when reefing.

rigging: ropes or cables used to support the masts and spars on a vessel (standing rigging) and to raise, lower, and control sails (running rigging).

raised deck: a deck created when cabin sides are brought out flush with the hull sides and the deck is raised so that it is on top of the cabin.

reverse transom: a transom the lines of which form an acute angle with the waterline.

scandalize: to reduce sail area, usually by topping the boom or lowering the peak of the sail.

self-bailing: with holes that permit water to drain out automatically.

set-up plank: a plank used in place of a keel, to which the frames and transom are attached on a sneakbox-type hull.

sheer: the longitudinal curve of the edge of the deck as seen from the side.

sheer strake: the top hull plank.

sheets: the lines used to trim the sails.

shrouds: the ropes or cables which support a mast.

skeg: (1) keel extension which may support the bottom of the rudder. (2) a short vertical appendage separate from the keel on which the rudder is hung.

spinnaker: large triangular sail used when running before the wind.

sprit: a small spar which crosses a fore and aft sail diagonally to extend it.

spritsail: a fore and aft sail extended by a sprit.

stem: a timber that extends up from the keel to form the bow of a vessel and to which the planking is fastened.

strake: a plank or continuous course of hull planking that reaches from bow to stern.

tiller: a bar attached to the rudder for steering a boat.

transom: the flat or curved stern face of the hull.

traveler: a rod on deck on which a ring slides, usually for the purpose of trimming sail.

vang: a line used to steady a spar. A boom vang is a line used to steady the boom when sailing before the wind.

weather helm: the tendency of a sailing craft to come up into the wind.

winch: a crank-driven drum used for trimming sail sheets.

wine glass keel: a type of keel characterized by a wine glass profile, section view.

wishbone, wishboom: a type of sprit consisting of two curved arms bolted together at both ends. The sail sets between the arms and its aerodynamic curve is not spoiled.

BIBLIOGRAPHY

Blanchard, Fessenden S. *The Sailboat Classes of North America.* Garden City, New York: Doubleday, 1968.

Brown, C. Pennington. "The North Haven Dinghies." *Down East,* August 1974, pp. 74–76.

Cheever, David, "The Herreshoff Fifteens." *The Log of Mystic Seaport,* Summer 1972.

Drinker, Pemberton. "Sneakbox." *WoodenBoat,* n. 20 (1978), pp. 23–26.

"Durable Bird Boats Celebrate 50th." *American Boating,* April 1972, pp. 32–34.

Erickson, Gene. "San Francisco Bay Birds Still Flying Despite Decades of Pounding." *National Fisherman,* August 1978, pp. 64–65.

Farrell, Jane. *The Wianno Senior.* privately published, 1969.

Guthorn, Peter J., M.D. *Seabright Skiff and Other Jersey Shore Boats.* Rutgers, New Jersey: Rutgers Press, 1971.

Harding, William G. "Renaissance of a Herreshoff Classic." *Sailing,* 1976.

Haskins, Sturgis. "Old design One-Designs live on in Maine." *National Fisherman,* January 1975.

———. "Still Racing at Sixty Plus." *Down East,* March 1974, pp. 70–71.

———. "Survival of the Fittest." *Yankee,* August 1972, p. 78.

Herreshoff Manufacturing Company. "Yachts by Herreshoff."

Horton, Annetta S. "SS One of the Oldest One-Design Classes." *Antique Boating,* Winter 1975, pp. 20–23.

Kimberly, James H. "The Inland Lake Scows." *Yachting,* March 1949.

Leavens, John M., ed. *The Catboat Book.* Camden, Maine: International Marine Publishing Company, 1973.

Medina, Standish F. *A History of the Westhampton Yacht Squadron 1890–1965.* privately published by the Westhampton Yacht Squadron, Ltd., 1965.

"More About the One-Design Classes." *Yachting,* March and April, 1947.

"Mr. Beetle Built a Boat." *Flying Your Way.* Air New England, Inc., Spring 1977.

Munro, Winthrop M. "Cape Cod's Baby Knockabout Grows Up." *Motorboating,* July 1961, p. 44.

"New Rig for Cape Cod Baby Knockabouts." *Yachting,* October 1936.

1972 Boat Owners Buyers Guide. New York: Yachting Publishing Corporation, 1971.

Ogilvy, C. Stanley. "50 Years of Stars." *Motor Boating,* May 1961.

"One Design Classes." *Rudder,* December 1911.

Phillips, W. Lyman. "The Same After 75 Years." *WoodenBoat,* March–April 1976.

Robinson, Bill. *The World of Yachting.* New York: Random House, 1966.

Schoettle, Edwin J., ed. *Sailing Craft.* New York: The Macmillan Company, 1928.

Slaughter, Samuel C. "Age Before Beauty." *Yachting,* July 1952.

Slaughter, Samuel C. "Three Score and Ten." *Yachting,* April 1959.

The Editors of Mechanix Illustrated. "Beetle Cats." *Sail Boating,* New York: Arco, 1959, pp. 104–108.

"They Never Say Die." *Yachting,* March 1966.

Trevor, John B., Jr. "The Unchallenged Idem." *Adirondack Life,* Summer 1972.

25th Anniversary 18' (Cape Cod Baby) Knockabout Class (Yearbook). Cape Cod Baby Knockabout Class Association, August 1962, pp. 2-10.

Welles, Edward R. III. "Grand Old One-Design." *Yachting,* July 1961, pp. 182–183.

———. "Grand Old One-Design Class Still Races off Northeast Harbor." *Down East,* September 1964, p. 32.

———. "History." *Mariners Notes and Antiques,* vol. 1, n. 4, 1977.

Wilson, Jon. "Concordia's Beetle Cat Shop." *WoodenBoat,* March–April 1978.